SARAH BROWN'S

WORLD VEGETARIAN

COOKBOOK

SARAH BROWN'S

WORLD VEGETARIAN COOKBOOK

VIKING
an imprint of
PENGUIN BOOKS

Viking

Penguin Group (Australia)
250 Camberwell Road, Camberwell, Victoria 3124, Australia
Penguin Books Ltd
80 Strand, London WC2R 0RL, England
Penguin Group (USA) Inc.
375 Hudson Street, New York, New York 10014, USA
Penguin Books, a division of Pearson Canada
10 Alcorn Avenue, Toronto, Ontario, Canada M4V 3B2
Penguin Books (NZ) Ltd
Cnr Rosedale and Airborne Roads, Albany, Auckland, New Zealand
Penguin Books (South Africa) (Pty) Ltd
24 Sturdee Avenue, Rosebank, Johannesburg 2196, South Africa
Penguin Books India (P) Ltd
11, Community Centre, Panchsheel Park, New Delhi 110 017, India

This edition published by Penguin Group (Australia),
a division of Pearson Group Pty Ltd, 2004

This book was conceived, designed, and produced by
THE IVY PRESS LIMITED
The Old Candlemakers,
West Street,
Lewes,
East Sussex, BN7 2NZ, UK

Creative Director PETER BRIDGEWATER
Publisher SOPHIE COLLINS
Editorial Director STEVE LUCK
Senior Project Editor REBECCA SARACENO
Design Manager TONY SEDDON
Designer JANE LANAWAY
Artwork Assistant JOANNA CLINCH
Photography CALVEY TAYLOR-HAW

Printed and bound in China

10 9 8 7 6 5 4 3 2 1

A CIP catalogue record for this book is available from the National Library of Australia

www.penguin.com.au

Dedication:
To Rachel Anderson and Rachel Skingsley, with love and thanks.

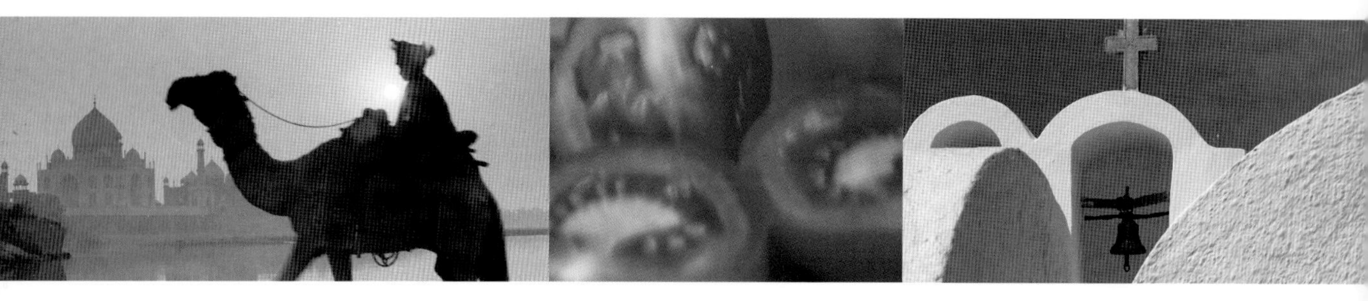

contents

introduction

First challenge: how to put the world into 100 recipes! My selection is a highly personal one and this book has allowed me to indulge two favourite pastimes, namely cooking and talking! My starting point was my friends from around the world who live both here in Britain and abroad. I quizzed them about favourite foods, things they cooked frequently, how dishes were flavoured and what went best with what. Everyone was so generous with their stories and suggestions. Some friends cooked for me here at home. Courtesy of the Internet there was some long-distance cooking in far-flung places such as India, as a flurry of e-mails flew through cyberspace.

Food is a useful barometer of the changing world in which we live. Many cities and towns are increasingly multicultural. London, where I live, is a good example with its many specialist shops and ethnic markets which sell an amazingly wide range of foods and where you can often get expert advice. Large supermarkets have an increasingly good choice of international foods with sections devoted to Japanese or Italian ingredients for example, or aisles stacked with an enormous choice of a basic ingredient such as rice. The latter now comes in brown, white, red and black as well as short-grain for risotto, delicate basmati and plump white grains for sticky rice. Out in the high street, restaurants too offer a choice of exotic food. Thai, Lebanese, Chinese, Indian, Turkish: the choice is fantastic. Even cooking in communities such as schools has more of a global feel than before.

In Indian cooking spices have many functions beyond flavouring: some colour, some thicken, some add heat and others a cooling element.

World food now comes to us in a number of ways – from tiny samosas and fragrant golden dips to stacks of freshly cooked tortillas and bright refreshing salsa, delicate sushi (always most beautifully displayed) and pitta bread with garlic-laden fillings. I've tasted and savoured, dipped and sampled, licked my lips and thought, I must find out how to make this.

Vegetables and grains form the staple diet in Africa, and bread is an indispensable part of the meal for mopping up sauces.

In the 100 recipes I've chosen, some 20 countries are represented and while the end result is an enormous variety of diverse dishes, most of the ingredients are readily available and pop up time and again. What I found fascinating was the numerous ways they are prepared, cooked and presented. The aubergine is a good example. In this book you'll find it succulently cooked in pistou, a gorgeous Spanish stew, roasted and puréed with garlic and herbs in a striking Lebanese dip, or stuffed with a spicy hot mixture from India and served with a richly aromatic coconut rice.

Cooking styles and techniques, too, alter the flavour of food. A soup cooked in the classic Greek style is gently simmered to bring out the very mellow flavour of the vegetables, then at the end olive oil and herbs are added to enhance the taste. Compare this with the classic olive-oil cooking in Turkey where ingredients are very slowly simmered in olive oil and their own juice for a strikingly different effect.

Interpreting recipes has had its funny moments. As many of us know with a favourite recipe, it gets an instinctive 'rightness' to it, and there's often no need to measure or weigh. My notes from conversations with cooks are full of 'a couple of handfuls', 'an enormous bunch', 'as much as fits in the pan' or 'a drizzle of oil' and so on. In one conversation I scribbled down some notes on garlic and then wasn't sure if I needed one clove or more. When I queried whether it was one or two, there was quite a pause while my friend considered and eventually said she felt two would be overdoing it, but added 'it depends on how big the bulbs are', and I realized her 'one' was not a clove of garlic at all but an entire head!

Using the recipes

Servings The majority of the recipes serve 4, but the servings or portions are given before each recipe.

Measurements are given in metric followed by imperial. Please note that you should follow only one set of measurements as they are not exactly compatible but rounded up or down to make realistic quantities. The conversions are standard, but are varied in one or two cases where the ratio of one ingredient to another is important, such as in pastry and breadmaking.

Standard level spoon measures are used:

1 tablespoon = one 15 ml spoon

1 teaspoon = one 5 ml spoon

Eggs are large unless otherwise stated

Vegetables are medium unless otherwise stated

Milk is full-fat unless otherwise stated

Many recipes have titles in the language of origin, so these are included where possible. The translation is not always direct and the title is written phonetically rather than exactly.

Flavouring with herbs and spices, both aromatic and hot, is fundamental to creating completely different tastes. Spice pastes, infusions, ground spices cooked slowly, roasted and sprinkled as a last-minute seasoning all add a different quality. In some countries, particular spices are favoured, such as the chilli in Asia and Latin America, sumac in the Middle East, cumin and black pepper in Morocco. Some fiery cocktails of garlic, chillies and ginger take time to get used to. If you are wary of spices, just go easy on the hot ingredients such as chilli.

The recipes in this book are grouped in six geographically organized sections which encompass the globe. In each section there is a general introduction to the region exploring common culinary links and key influences. Sometimes I've described an individual country, giving more details on particular elements in that cuisine.

In each section there are two special pages highlighting key elements. Some of these feature pages focus on ingredients, such as the coconut used in much of Asia, the pulses used widely in the Indian subcontinent, or the chilli which dominates many Latin American dishes. Some of the feature pages look at styles of eating such as the mezze from the Middle East or tapas – tiny appetizers from Spain. Other feature pages include recipes for a typical dish with tips on variations and troubleshooting, such as the muffins and cookies of America, or classic pastry making in Europe.

Within each section, there is a range of distinctive recipes including starters, main courses and light meals, and sometimes side vegetables, salads, breads, baking and desserts.

Overall, I've tried to include recipes that appeal in a universal sense. This generally means, not too long to prepare or with too long a list of ingredients. Whilst it's fun trying some weird and wonderful dish, if at the end of the day it has tiny amounts of several obscure ingredients or something like three days of fermentation needed, it's a non-starter.

I also homed in on recipes that were vegetarian at source rather than adaptations. Over the years I've written many recipes for classic dishes adjusted to suit vegetarians, but I thought this was an opportunity for less meddling from me and a way of leading to some wonderful new dishes.

In any of the sections you can create a whole meal or use one or two ideas for just one course or snack, or mix and match using food from different sections. Whatever you choose, I hope you will enjoy meals from these recipes, get many new ideas and bring a truly foreign flavour to your table.

A visit to the fresh food markets of Asia can be an exhilarating and colourful experience: invariably they offer a whole host of different food items you may not have seen before.

americas

This section includes mainly food from Mexico and Colombia and savouries from the southern states of North America. There are of course countless other recipes available from all over Latin America, far beyond the scope of this book, so I've also flagged up several favourite flavourings which are really intended to whet the appetite for anyone able to explore these regions further.

I love the colourful exuberant food of Mexico, a vibrant array of sweet and hot peppers and glossy chillies, bright green coriander, fragrant tangy limes and rich golden corn. The food served here makes a great starting point as it is easy and enticing. Many of the well-known recipes such as guacamole, *huevos rancheros* (fried eggs in a spicy salsa), refried beans, and other simple dishes served with corn tortillas are immediately appealing. Small wonder that Mexican food has achieved such worldwide popularity. What I also enjoy is its very free style in that one basic dish can have almost endless variations. Take the melted cheese with mushrooms on page 25. It can be eaten with no more than a few torn pieces of tortilla and a dollop of cream, with both raw and cooked salsas, spicy or not as you wish, pressed into home-made tortillas to make appetizing bites, or served with rice and topped with some chargrilled mild chillies.

My favourite kitchen tool at the moment is a huge chunk of rather unprepossessing stone, a small piece of a volcano in actual fact, called a *metlapil e molcajete*, which is the Mexican equivalent of a pestle and mortar. The *metlapil* is the traditional implement used for grinding or pounding ingredients. One minute you have in front of you a couple of cloves of garlic, a chilli, some onion and coriander. A quick grind of salt and a few turns of the wrist and the ingredients begin to blend into a flavourful sauce. If you're ever lucky enough to go to Mexico and are prepared to carry back some heavy baggage, I can recommend a *metlapil e molcajete*: it's a joy to use.

salsas and staples

Salsas can enliven a host of savoury dishes, from plainly cooked beans to chilli stews, and simple fried vegetables such as mushrooms. Salsas work as dips, dressings and relishes. The tradition of the salsa runs throughout Latin America and here I've included a favourite from Argentina, chimichurri, an aromatic relish with flat parsley or coriander, lemon and shallots. Look on page 23 for some inspiration.

Golden corn has been a staple of the Mexican diet for over 4,000 years. The kernels are softened in water and lime juice and then ground and usually made into tortillas. These are fun to make and there's a recipe on page 25. Protein-rich beans such as pinto beans and kidney beans add substance, and dozens of different chillies provide the flavour base along with a fabulous array of fruits and vegetables: tomatoes, squash, sweet potatoes, avocado, coconut, pineapple and papaya. I've included a classic chilli (*page 27*) using some of the favoured Mexican spices such as cinnamon and cumin, but you can also try cloves or aniseed as well as fresh herbs such as coriander, thyme, marjoram and the pungent *epazote*.

Travellers through Mexico can also sample the many regional variations of Mexican food. Northern cooking tends to use grilling and charring methods, which add elusive smoky flavours to the food. In central Mexico, there is a more obvious Spanish influence alongside the native Indian staples. The south is heavily influenced by native Indian cultures. Recipes from this region incorporate numerous dried peppers in stews and sauces to wake up the taste buds, as well as sweeter spices, such as cinnamon and cloves, which act as a foil to the fiery flavours.

There is also a sweet side to Mexican life as sugar arrived in Mexico at about the same time as the Conquest. The ancient Mexicans liked the taste of sweet food and sweetened their drinks and desserts with honey, cactus fruits and corn syrup. Many sweet products are made for traditional holidays such as the Day of the Dead with its famous sugar skulls.

The bold colourful style throughout Latin America shows a blending of native traditions and the influence of the generally European explorers and invaders. A strong Spanish influence comes from the early settlers, who brought cumin, oregano, cinnamon and aniseed. There is also widespread use of fresh orange and lime juices, often combined with the great Mediterranean standbys of wine and olive oil. Many dishes make very imaginative combinations of sweet and salty flavours, for example, using sweet raisins with salted capers and olives. As a contrast I've included a delicious simple Colombian recipe for a breakfast soup (*page 17*) which I'm assured is a great cure for a hangover!

Peru has some of the spiciest food in South America. The preferred seasoning here is the *aji amarillo*, a fiery yellow chilli that adds bite to everything. It was here, too, that the potato originated and Peruvians can now boast of some 300 different varieties. I can't resist detailing one method of preparation even though it is impossible to replicate! It dates back to Inca times. The potato is squeezed to get rid of most of the moisture but retain its shape. It is put in the snow for a week, then left in hot sun until completely dried out. Once dried, apparently it keeps for 50 years, so I suppose it is the ultimate store-cupboard standby.

Brazil has a diverse cuisine revealing African, Indian and Portuguese influences, very much reflecting the history of the region. Beans make a daily appearance on the table in many forms and an array of colours. The black bean holds pride of place as the national bean and is frequently made into *feijoada*, a simmered stew. Created originally as a simple dish using left-overs, this recipe works equally well served with extra vegetables to make a robust hearty meal. Another firm favourite is the rice and bean dish, *arroz-feijao*, which, depending on the locality, can be made using red, black or white beans

I've also included the soup or stew known as gumbo, traditionally served with cornbread (*page 30*), from the southern states of North America. The food influences here reflect both Cajun and Creole traditions. Cajun cooking comes from an area west of New Orleans originally settled by colonizers of French descent in the 1700s. Later, the Spaniards brought spices with peppers and seasoning, cayenne in particular, and from Africa came the introduction of okra and sweet potatoes. New Orleans itself, the heart of Creole cookery, is also a remarkable blend of national influences, not only French and Spanish but also African, Portuguese and West Indian.

To round off this section, there are also two gorgeous desserts and a feature on baking, including recipes for raspberry and cinammon muffins and pecan cookies (*pages 40–41*).

common ingredients and useful techniques

avocado

Hass is one of the most popular varieties of avocado grown in Mexico. It is medium-sized with very dark green, almost black, rough skin. A ripe avocado will yield gently when pressed. If bought unripe, it will ripen at home. To speed up this process, put in a paper bag for a day or so. Do not refrigerate or it will turn black.

cheese

Mexican cheeses tend to be quite crumbly and salty. *Queso fresco*, probably the most widely known Mexican cheese, has an off-white colour and a crumbly texture that melts easily. Try using Cheshire or feta. For melting, Cheddar is fine, or mozzarella for delicious moist strings.

coriander

Fresh coriander, with its distinctive pungent-tasting green leaves, is used in vast amounts for salsas, stirred into cooked beans, and for flavouring soup. This herb will keep fresh for about a week in the refrigerator if you cut off the lower stems and wrap in kitchen paper.

corn (sweetcorn/corn on the cob)

Fresh corn on the cob goes well with flavourings such as lime and chilli. It can also be bought canned or frozen, but the best flavour comes from stripping the fresh cob of its kernels. To do this, hold the cob at an angle with the tip pressed on a firm surface and cut downwards with a sharp knife. Sweetcorn kernels add good colour and texture to stews, grain dishes and salads.

herbs

Most of the common herbs used in South America such as basil, parsley, bay leaf, oregano and thyme are well known and easily accessible. *Epazote*, a pungent herb with a strong taste, is used in central and southern Mexico but is not widely available outside the country.

lime

This fragrant citrus fruit goes well with chilli, fresh coriander, avocado and tomatoes. Use it to add a tang to salsa and salad dressings.

maize and *masa harina*

Native to America, corn is ground into flour to make a range of delicious quick cornbreads. *Masa harina* is a flour made from corn that has been cooked with slaked lime, then dried and ground to a flour, which gives it a distinctive taste and smell.

okra

This unusual five-sided, tapered, oblong vegetable is used extensively in the southern states of America. The cut pods release a slippery gelatinous juice, which thickens a soup or stew as well as adding a mild flavour.

tomatillos

Although tomato-like in appearance, tomatillos are not green tomatoes but a relative of the Cape gooseberry. Concealed in a dry papery husk, tomatillos are pale green with a tart fresh flavour.

stuffing

Corn tortillas, the staple pancake-like breads, are the basis for many dishes, and are served in various ways:

Burritos: stuffed tortilla parcels

Enchiladas: tortillas dipped in chilli sauce, filled and baked

Quesadillas: folded with cheese and fried

Tacos: warmed tortillas stuffed and eaten soft

Tostadas: crisp fried tortillas topped with chilli or beans

Tortilla chips: tortillas cut into wedges and deep-fried

chopping

To cube or dice a spring onion very finely, hold the bulb in your hand and use a very sharp knife (take great care!) to lightly slice it in fine cuts, then again at right angles. Place the bulb on a board and chop off the cut sections. Repeat until you have cut down to the green part.

grinding

Mexican pestles and mortars made from rough, non-porous, dark grey or black volcanic rock can be anything from hand-size to the size of a small table. The *metlapil e molcajete* is the traditional implement found in all Mexican kitchens and is used to grind corn and chillies, spices and seeds, and to create salsas. The slow grinding creates an even texture and intensifies the flavours in a way that is different from an electric grinder.

measuring

Use a set of cup measures to get the right volume quickly, without having to weigh out.

colombian breakfast

changua

This is a delicately flavoured soup from Colombia. It is served at breakfast and meant to be a fantastic cure for a hangover. It is simple to make but it is important to chop both the spring onions and coriander finely so they impart maximum flavour. Spring onions in South America are much larger than the European varieties, more like a baby leek but with a milder flavour; generally only the whites are used. Unusually, they are chopped across the top and then again at right angles, then placed on a board and chopped vertically. Using this method, you get minute squares which look very attractive.

SERVES 4

8 large spring onions, white bulbs only, diced
1 tbsp olive oil
600ml (1 pint) milk
4 tbsp water
8 tbsp finely chopped fresh coriander
salt and pepper
4 eggs
2 slices French toast or crusty baguette

1 Finely dice the spring onion bulbs (*see page 15* for a description of the technique). Heat the oil in a medium pan and quickly fry the onions not to colour but just soften. Pour on the milk and water and stir in half the coriander. Heat the mixture slowly until it is just below boiling point, seasoning well. It is important not to let the milk boil or the flavour of the soup will change.

2 Break in the eggs, putting them very gently into the mixture and then letting them poach for 2–3 minutes. Once the eggs are cooked, crumble in the bread and sprinkle over the remaining coriander.

red onion and yellow pepper chowder

The name 'chowder' comes from the French word *chaudière*, meaning kettle or cauldron. Having travelled across the Atlantic, chowders were initially hearty soups containing, as one would expect along a coastline, seafood. As the early settlers moved inland, many variations of this basic recipe were made with numerous additions as wide-ranging as beer, green peppers, milk or Tabasco. This version uses colourful, succulent red onions and yellow peppers cooked very slowly with potato to give a thick, satisfying texture. It is more of a soup than a stew but eaten with bread makes a good meal.

SERVES 4

2 tbsp olive oil
2 red onions, finely diced
1 clove garlic, chopped
1 stick celery, diced
1 large carrot diced
1 large yellow pepper, deseeded and diced
2 small new potatoes, scrubbed and chopped
3 tomatoes, chopped
1 tsp dried thyme
1 bay leaf
2 tbsp finely chopped parsley
600ml (1 pint) vegetable stock
salt and pepper
1 tbsp finely chopped parsley, for garnish

1 Heat the oil in a medium pan and gently fry the onions and garlic until soft.

2 Add the celery, carrot and yellow pepper and cook for about 10 minutes until fairly soft.

3 Add the potatoes, tomatoes, thyme, bay leaf, parsley and also the vegetable stock.

4 Bring to the boil, cover, and simmer for 35–40 minutes or until the vegetables are very tender. Mash the potato in the pan to give the soup a thicker texture.

5 Season to taste and serve garnished with parsley.

COOK'S TIP *Other vegetables can be used, such as chopped green beans or a variety of coloured peppers.*

chillies

Cultivated in Latin America, the West Indies and the Far East, the numerous types of chilli come in different sizes, colours and fieriness. Red chillies are riper than green chillies and have a fuller flavour and can taste slightly sweeter.

heat scale

Surprisingly it was over 100 years ago that the heat scale for chillies was developed by Scoville. It measured the strength of capsaicin, the chemical that produces the fiery sensation. Large bell peppers are measured as zero, with the hottest, the habañero, going up to 10,000-plus units. As a rough guide the smaller and narrower the chilli and the darker its colour, the more powerful its heat. Chillies can add a wonderful dimension to your cooking, creating sensations from a rich warmth to a dramatic heat. When you can't get a particular chilli you can substitute another sort that has an equivalent heat scale rating.

buying and storing

Look for bright glossy skins and avoid any chillies that are bruised. Chillies can be stored for up to 3 weeks in the refrigerator. Remove any with mould as this spreads quickly. Chillies can also be covered in oil, to keep the air out, and kept in a cool place.

Today chillies are grown around the world, from the Far East through India to Mexico.

preparation

Always treat chillies with care as they contain oils that can permeate the skin. It is a good idea to wear disposable gloves and, after chopping a chilli, never touch your eyes or mouth. Wash your hands thoroughly as well as the knife and chopping board. All of the chilli's heat is concentrated in the seeds and ribs. To lessen the heat just remove all or some of these parts.

roast chilli

This can be done in the oven or under the grill. Roast or grill the chilli until the skin is charred. Peel the skin off while the chilli is still warm. With thin-skinned chillies, particularly green ones, once roasted put them in a polythene bag and leave for 10 minutes to steam. They should then be easier to peel.

rehydrating dried chilli

Cover in boiling water and leave for 15–30 minutes. Drain and crush in a pestle and mortar or purée in a blender. You can also fry them in a little oil until they puff up, or lightly roast them. Alternatively, first toast dry chillies under a hot grill for 2–3 minutes. Make sure you work in a well-ventilated room while doing this as the chilli can release volatile oils that may sting your eyes.

dried chilli flakes

These are a very useful store-cupboard ingredient and save chopping.

Some of the most popular chilli types:

anaheim

This mild green chilli can be roasted and stuffed. It has a fresh green taste with medium to thick flesh, improved by charring or roasting.

ancho

These are dried poblano chillies, dark reddish brown, fairly mild, with a complex flavour of liquorice, tobacco, coffee and raisins. Used in mole, enchilada sauces, tamales and stews.

habañero

Closely related to the Scotch bonnet, these are one of the hottest chillies you can get. Behind the heat is a fruity flavour.

jalapeño

Popular in Mexico, this green chilli is fairly hot with a clean taste. It is also good pickled or grilled and stuffed. Once dried and smoked, the jalapeño takes on the name of chipotle.

kenyan

These small green chillies are similar to jalapeño and range from medium hot to hot.

poblano

This relatively mild, thick-fleshed, dark green chilli flavours many Mexican dishes. It can also be stuffed. Roasting gives it a smokier flavour.

serrano

A thick-fleshed, bullet-shaped chilli with a clean fresh green flavour and blistering heat. It turns from light green to red and is used in many bottled chilli sauces.

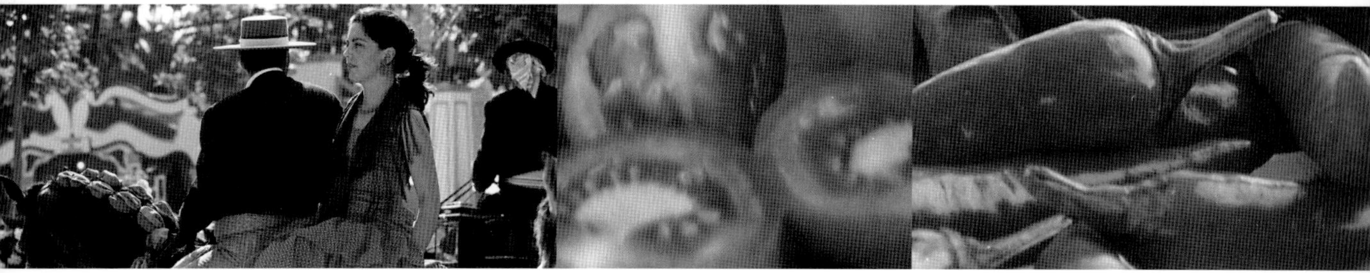

salsa

'Salsa' is the Spanish word for sauce and in Mexico, the principal ingredients that make a salsa are finely chopped onions, garlic and tomatoes, with extras such as chillies, coriander and lime. Salsas can be fresh or cooked, with flavours from mild to spicy, tangy or pungent. For a richer salsa, use some chopped avocado or make one that is more refreshing by adding tropical fruit such as mango or papaya.

mexican salsa

salsa mexicana

This is the classic salsa made simply from onion, tomatoes and coriander. Chop the ingredients to approximately the same size. Once you have made the basic dish, you can try adding chopped chilli (red or green), lime juice or extra garlic to ring the changes.

1 small onion, finely chopped
1 clove garlic, finely chopped
4 tomatoes, finely chopped
2–3 tbsp chopped fresh coriander
salt

Prepare all the ingredients, mix together and season with salt.

'Salsa makes a great appetizer. Here are a few classic ideas to start you off.'

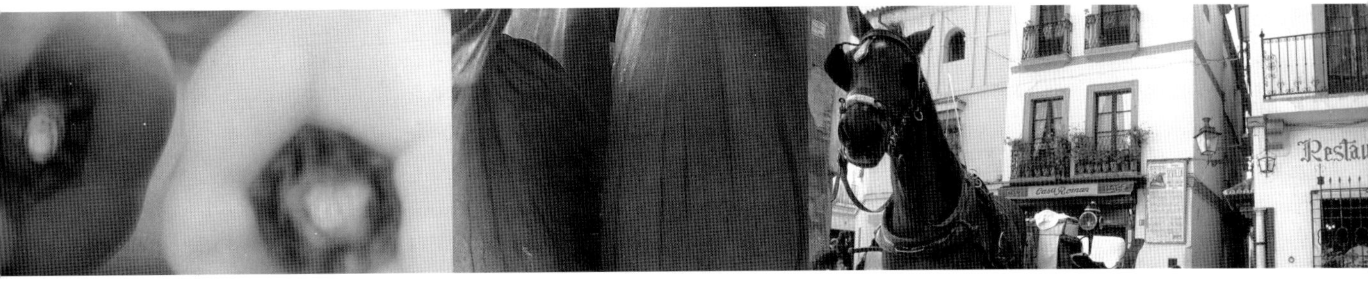

green salsa

salsa verde

The greenness of this salsa comes from the tomatillo known also as *tomate verde* which is grown extensively in Mexico and South America. The tomatillo has a soft green flesh (similar in colour to gooseberries) with a clean taste. The fruit has a thin papery husk which is easily removed. For a less spicy version, omit the chilli.

4 tomatillos
1 clove garlic, finely chopped
1 green chilli, deseeded and chopped
2–3 tbsp chopped fresh coriander
salt

Remove the husks from the tomatillos, chop finely and mix with the remaining ingredients. Season with salt.

avocado salsa

avocado salsa

This is a mild, fruity salsa with an attractive combination of colours.

1 red pepper, deseeded and diced
1 ripe avocado, peeled and diced
1 papaya, peeled and diced
juice of 1/2 lime
2 tbsp chopped fresh coriander
salt

Prepare all the ingredients and gently mix together. Season with salt.

herb salsa

chimichurri

This is an intense green herb salsa from Argentina. Other herbs such as thyme and oregano can be added and the sauce can be spiced with a little cayenne if you wish.

125ml (4fl oz) olive oil
2 tbsp fresh lemon juice
3–4 tbsp finely chopped fresh flat-leaf parsley or coriander
1 clove garlic, finely chopped
2 shallots, finely chopped
salt

Combine all ingredients and season. Leave to stand before serving for the flavour to develop.

marinated vegetables

verduras en escabeche

This is a typical Mexican starter that lends itself to numerous variations, but will naturally include chillies and garlic! Serve cold as a starter alongside a bowl of olives or use the vegetables in other dishes. One or two of the peppers are great finely chopped and scattered over a quesadilla or used in any melted cheese dish.

SERVES 4–6

- 4–5 tbsp olive oil
- 1 onion, cut in rings
- 4–6 cloves garlic, peeled and left whole
- 8–10 firm chillies, medium heat, sliced lengthways
- 3 carrots, sliced in rings
- 1 small cauliflower, divided into florets
- 350g (12oz) button mushrooms
- 125ml (4fl oz) white wine vinegar
- 1 bay leaf
- 8 peppercorns
- 1 tsp oregano
- salt and pepper

1 Heat the olive oil in a pan and gently fry the onion and garlic without colouring.

2 Add the chillies, carrots and cauliflower and cook on a medium heat for 2–3 minutes to coat with oil and seal in the flavour. Add the mushrooms and cook briefly until coated with a little oil.

3 Pour over the wine vinegar and add the bay leaf, peppercorns and oregano then season well. Cook for 2–3 minutes and then remove the pan from the heat.

4 Leave to cool completely then pile into a bowl and serve with cocktail sticks so the individual pieces can be speared.

5 The vegetables can also be put in a clean jar with a good seal and stored for some months.

melted cheese with mushrooms

queso fundido con champiñones

The array of simple tasty dishes from Mexico are great for simple suppers and informal entertaining. Tortillas, salsas and soured cream are your basics: try grilled peppers, roasted tomatoes or this tasty recipe to ring the changes.

SERVES 4

FOR THE TOPPING

2 tbsp olive oil
1 onion, finely diced
250g (8oz) button mushrooms, sliced
1–2 cloves garlic, finely chopped
50–75g (2–3oz) grated mild cheese (*see page 14*)

TO SERVE

tortillas
salsa (*see pages 22–23*)

1 In a frying pan, heat the oil and fry the onion until soft. Add the mushrooms and garlic and cook until the mushroom slices are soft and very lightly browned.

2 Sprinkle over the grated cheese and cover with a lid, leave on a very low heat until the cheese has melted.

3 To serve spoon the mushroom mixture onto a tortilla, and top with salsa.

4 Alternatively, to make mushroom quesadilla, sandwich mushroom filling between two tortillas, return to the frying pan and press down on the tortilla and cook until the tortilla is crisp. Cut into wedges and serve topped with salsa and soured cream.

tortillas

MAKES 12

250g (8oz) maize flour
300–350ml (10–12fl oz) warm water

> COOK'S TIP *Tortillas are simple to make but you do need a good maize flour* (masa harina), *available from specialist shops or suppliers. If you can't find it, it may be wiser to buy ready made tortillas.*

1 Put the maize flour in a large bowl and mix in the warm water to make a soft dough.

2 Cover the bowl with clingfilm, or a cloth and leave to rest for about 10–15 minutes.

3 Divide the dough into 12 pieces and roll each one out into a ball.

4 Pat each ball into a small round keeping the dough an even thickness.

5 Heat a heavy frying pan and when hot, put in the tortilla and cook for 1–2 minutes on either side or until the outer surface of the dough looks dry and a bit speckled.

6 Keep the cooked tortillas warm in a napkin-lined basket while you cook the remaining dough.

chilli

Chillis are wonderful robust stews which go well with a great range of simple colourful accompaniments. This recipe uses a range of spices loosely based on the famous 'mole' sauce from Mexico where some 16 or more ingredients including chillies, spices and bitter chocolate are mixed together to produce a rich, rounded flavour.

SERVES 4–6

3 tbsp olive oil
3 onions, roughly chopped
4 cloves garlic, crushed
1 red chilli, deseeded and diced
1 tsp dried thyme
1 tsp allspice
1 cinnamon stick
3 tsp ground cumin
25g (1oz) chocolate
2 sticks celery, sliced
3 medium carrots, peeled and chopped
1 green pepper, chopped
250g (8oz) pinto beans, cooked weight or 1 x 400g (14oz) can pinto beans, rinsed and drained
250g (8oz) red kidney beans, cooked weight or 1 x 400g (14oz) can red kidney beans, rinsed and drained
2 x 400g (14oz) cans chopped tomatoes
salt and pepper

TO SERVE

soured cream; salsa of spring onions, avocado and fresh coriander; soft tortillas, grated cheese

1 In a large pan or casserole, heat the oil and gently fry the onion and garlic until soft but not coloured.

2 Add the chilli, thyme, allspice, cinnamon, and cumin to the pan and fry for about 2 minutes.

3 Then stir in the chocolate and let it melt.

4 Add the celery, carrot and green pepper and cook slowly for 7–10 minutes. Then add the beans and mix in well and cook for a further 4–5 minutes. Then add the canned tomatoes and bring the mixture to the boil. Season well, cover the pan and simmer for 40–50 minutes, stirring occasionally.

5 Adjust the seasoning and serve hot with a range of accompaniments such as soured cream, grated cheese, soft tortillas, or a salsa of chopped spring onions, avocado and fresh coriander.

corn and leek strata

There are several recipes from Bermuda where vegetables are layered with breadcrumbs and herbs and baked. I think they are particularly successful when the breadcrumbs are used to make a crust and the vegetables are cooked in a savoury custard. The dish can be prepared well ahead as it needs to stand before cooking. The end result is a moist well-flavoured savoury dish that can be served with a crisp green salad or simple steamed vegetables.

SERVES 4

6 slices wholemeal bread
15g (½oz) butter
2 leeks, cleaned and chopped
2 courgettes, sliced
1 cob sweetcorn, kernels stripped
4 eggs
450ml (15fl oz) milk
1 tsp dried thyme
125g (4oz) grated Cheddar cheese
salt and pepper

1 Butter the bread, (you can trim the crust if you wish) and use the slices to line the base and sides of a lightly buttered 17x28-cm (7x11-inch) baking dish.

2 Lightly steam or grill the courgettes and leeks for about 5 minutes or until just tender.

3 Sprinkle the corn kernels over the buttered bread and then arrange the courgettes and leeks in a layer over the top.

4 Beat the eggs lightly with the milk and stir in the thyme. Season well. Pour the egg mixture over the vegetables and sprinkle over the grated cheese.

5 Cover and refrigerate for 4 hours or more.

6 Bake at 190°C (375°F) Gas Mark 5 for 45–50 minutes or until the top feels firm to the touch.

7 Leave to stand for 5 minutes before serving.

gumbo with cheese cornbread

Gumbo is a soup or stew from the southern states of America, generally containing okra. This vegetable has a silky quality and acts as a thickener for the stew. Served with a simple cheese cornbread, this makes a tasty meal.

SERVES 4

2 tbsp sunflower oil
3 shallots, finely chopped
2 cloves garlic, crushed
2 green peppers, deseeded and diced
2 sticks celery, chopped
250g (8oz) okra, chopped
450g (¾ pint) passata
1 bay leaf
¼ tsp cayenne
salt and pepper

1 Heat the oil in a pan and gently cook the shallots and garlic until soft, then add the peppers, celery and okra and mix well. Cook for 10 minutes over a slow heat so that the pepper begins to soften.

2 Pour over the passata and add the bay leaf and cayenne. Bring to the boil and cook for 25–30 minutes, adding a little water if necessary. Season to taste for the topping

cheese cornbread muffins

MAKES 12

75g (3oz) corn meal or maize flour
75g (3oz) wholemeal or white flour
½ tsp salt
1½ tsp baking powder
1 egg
150ml (¼ pint) milk
75g (3oz) Cheddar cheese, grated

1 To make the muffins, in a large bowl, mix the corn meal with the flour, salt and baking powder.

2 In a bowl, beat the egg with the milk and pour over the dry ingredients. Mix until just combined.

3 Spoon the batter into muffin cases and fill about ⅔ full. Bake at 200°C (400°F) Gas Mark 6 for 12–15 minutes.

4 Serve warm with the gumbo.

baked harlequin squash with wild rice

Wild rice, a slender mahogany coloured grain with its faintly salty tang, was originally native to the Great Lakes of North America, but it is now grown more widely. It can be served on its own but I think it is brilliant when combined with succulent vegetables as it lends both a dramatic colour and a good texture.

SERVES 4

50g (2oz) wild rice
4 harlequin or onion squash
2 tbsp sunflower or olive oil
350g (12oz) leeks, cleaned and finely chopped
25g (1oz) walnuts, chopped
pinch of nutmeg
300ml (10fl. oz) double cream
salt and pepper

1 Cook the wild rice in plenty of boiling water for 35–40 minutes or until the grains have cracked open and curled. Drain and leave to cool.

2 Slice the 'lid' off the top of each squash and remove the seeds and cut away a little of the flesh, leaving a thick shell. Reserve the flesh. Cut a little slice off the base of each squash so that the shells do not wobble. Season the inside of each shell.

3 Heat the oil in a large pan and gently fry the leeks for a few minutes, then stir in the squash flesh, chopped walnuts, nutmeg and cooked wild rice. Season well. Divide the vegetables into the squash shells and pour over the cream. Cover with the lids.

4 Bake at 180°C (350°F) Gas Mark 4 for 35–45 minutes. Serve hot.

COOK'S TIP *Use different baby squashes as they come into season, such as onion squash or acorn squash.*

grilled mushroom salad with crisp greens and walnuts

This can be a side salad or a light lunch or supper dish. Choose fresh crisp greens such as iceberg or cos lettuce and for a sharper touch use a few blades of white chicory. Don't swamp the salad in dressing, coat the grilled mushrooms and then drizzle over extra dressing, serve the rest in a small bowl as a side dip.

SERVES 4

FOR THE DRESSING
6 tbsp olive oil
2 tbsp soured cream
2 tsp white vinegar
½ tsp mustard
75g (3oz) blue cheese

FOR THE SALAD
3 large field mushrooms
oil for brushing
75g (3oz) walnut pieces
salad leaves such as iceberg, cos, chicory and watercress
salt and pepper

1 To make the dressing, mix the oil, soured cream, wine vinegar and mustard together until creamy and smooth. Then mash in the blue cheese to make a coarsely textured dressing. Season to taste.

2 Brush the mushrooms with oil and season with pepper (salt makes them a bit watery) then grill for 4–5 minutes or until soft. Slice thinly and cool. Lightly toast the walnuts under the grill for a minute.

3 Prepare the salad leaves and just before serving, dip the mushroom slices in the dressing and pile on top of the salad, scatter over the walnut pieces and drizzle over a little extra dressing or serve that separately.

TIMESAVER *The blue cheese dressing can be made in advance. It also makes a delicious dip for raw vegetables.*

coleslaw

The great thing about coleslaw (apart from being delicious) is that it is a salad that lends itself to travelling, or standing before being served, which makes it very useful for barbecues and picnics. I think it's a salad too easily overlooked because often it is associated with over-sweetened, sloppy, commercially made mixtures. Make your own. It is easy and well worth it. Try adding smoked pimenton which will give the coleslaw a peppery kick.

SERVES 4–6

FOR THE DRESSING

150ml (5fl oz) soured cream
100ml (3½oz) mayonnaise
1 tbsp white wine vinegar
1 tsp caraway seeds
1 tsp fresh dill, chopped
¼–½ tsp smoked pimenton

FOR THE SALAD

450g (1lb) firm white cabbage
1 green pepper, deseeded and finely sliced
2 carrots, grated
3 spring onions, finely chopped
1 crisp dessert apple, diced
salt and pepper
25g (1oz) pumpkin seeds, to garnish

1 Prepare the dressing by mixing together all the ingredients and season to taste.

2 Discard the outer leaves of the cabbage and cut out the tough core, then shred the remainder finely. A slicing blade on a food processor should make the task easier.

3 Prepare the other vegetables and the apple and then mix everything together in a large bowl.

4 Stir in the dressing until the whole salad is evenly coasted. Adjust the seasoning and leave to stand for a while for the flavours to develop. Garnish with pumpkin seeds before serving.

TIMESAVER *Using a food processor takes the labour out of chopping the cabbage and greatly speeds up the preparation.*

passion fruit and strawberry meringue

This recipe really spans the Pacific, it takes as a base the soft sticky pavlova-style meringues of Australia and is filled with the intensely perfumed passion fruit of South America, vanilla, cream and strawberries.

SERVES 6–8

4 large egg whites
2 tbsp cold water
225g (8oz) sugar
1 tsp vinegar
1 tsp vanilla extract
1 tsp cornflour
pinch of salt

FOR THE FILLING

4 passion fruits
1 tbsp caster sugar
icing sugar, for dusting
300ml (10fl oz) double cream
400g (14oz) strawberries

1 In a large bowl, beat the egg whites until stiff but not dry.

2 Add the water and beat again, then add the sugar a little at a time beating thoroughly until the sugar is dissolved.

3 Sprinkle over the vinegar, vanilla extract, cornflour and salt. Beat again.

4 Spoon the mixture onto a Swiss roll tin lined with baking parchment or greaseproof paper.

5 Bake the roulade base for 15 minutes at 180°C (350°F) Gas Mark 4, then turn off the oven and leave the meringue to cool completely covered with a slightly damp piece of greaseproof paper.

6 When cold, flip the roulade out onto a clean sheet of parchment.

7 For the filling, scoop out the flesh from the passion fruits and place in a small saucepan and add the tablespoon of sugar. Heat through until the sugar has dissolved but do not boil, then sieve the mixture and leave to cool.

8 Slice 300g (10oz) strawberries, leaving the rest for decoration.
Whip the cream and fold in 2–3 tablespoons of the passion fruit syrup. Spread the cream over the meringue base and cover with sliced strawberries. Roll up the meringue starting from the short end.

9 Dust with icing sugar and decorate with the remaining strawberries.
Serve in slices pouring over any remaining passion fruit sauce.

Gigantic crumbly cookies and softly domed muffins are mouth-watering examples of classic American baking. Both of these recipes are open to endless variations and are very quick to make. You'll find the American-style muffins are a cross between a bread and a cake.

raspberry and cinnamon muffins

Muffins are very easy to make. It is generally a matter of mixing wet and dry ingredients. The secret being not to over mix but just stir until the ingredients are combined. For this reason I prefer to use frozen raspberries (even in the height of summer) as they are easier to mix and don't disintegrate. The other tip about muffins, is to eat them straight away!

MAKES 12

250g (8oz) plain flour
150g (5oz) soft brown sugar
2 tsp baking powder
¼ tsp salt
1½ tsp cinnamon
1 egg, beaten
250ml (8fl oz) milk
50g (2oz) melted butter or 50ml (2fl oz) sunflower oil
150g (5oz) frozen or fresh raspberries

1 In a large bowl, mix together the flour, sugar, baking powder, salt and cinnamon.

2 In a separate bowl, mix together the egg, milk and melted butter or oil.

3 Then pour the milk and egg mixture over the dry ingredients adding the frozen or fresh raspberries at the same time and stir together, only mixing until just combined.

4 Spoon into 12 muffin cases filling each case about ⅔ full and bake at 200°C (400°F) Gas Mark 6 for 25 minutes or until firm and springy to the touch.

5 Cool in the cases on a wire rack.

pecan cookies

These are melt in the mouth made in a moment cookies that sometimes never even reach the cookie tin they are gone so fast in our house. Once you feel confident and quick with this recipe, try your own variations by adding different nuts, a range of sugars, extra spices such as ginger or cinnamon or a little grated lemon or orange zest.

MAKES ABOUT 30

250g (8oz) butter
150g (5oz) soft brown sugar
2 eggs
$^{1}/_{2}$ tsp vanilla extract
250g (8oz) flour
1 tsp baking powder
pinch of salt
75–100g (3–3$^{1}/_{2}$oz) pecan nuts, chopped

1 In a large bowl, cream the butter and sugar until pale.

2 Beat in the eggs and add the vanilla extract.

3 Sift in the flour, baking powder and salt. Then fold the chopped pecan nuts into the mixture.

4 Spoon walnut size dollops onto two lightly greased baking sheets, spacing the dollops out as they will spread.

5 Bake the cookies at 180°C (350°F) Gas Mark 4 for 9–12 minutes or until very pale brown.

6 Cool on a wire rack.

basic muffins

The trick with muffins is not to over mix. Stir the wet and dry ingredients briefly to keep the mixture light.

To do this, put all the dry ingredients in one bowl and in another bowl mix all the wet ingredients. Then mix the two, but only until dry ingredients are moistened, even leaving some lumps.

Spoon the mixture into muffin cases and bake until well risen. The finished muffin should feel light for its size and when broken open, be moist and tender inside.

Muffins are best eaten the day they are made. Should you have any left over, they freeze well.

cookies

Cookies are also fast and easy to make. Generally they are a simple combination of flour, butter, sugar, eggs, baking powder/soda and flavourings.

With electric whisks and processors, it is easy to mix the batter in one stage. As with muffins, don't over mix, but just combine the ingredients until the batter is smooth. Don't over bake cookies as they will become dry and hard. The time needed to cook will vary depending on whether you are making tablespoon-sized drops or saucer like discs.

As you start making variations to suit your taste, it is useful to look out for the following. If your cookies spread out too much, it may be that the dough is too soft. You can try adding a little more flour or putting the dough in the refrigerator for 15 minutes or so to firm. If the cookies brown too quickly but the insides don't cook, this may be due to having too much sugar in the mixture.

Very dry cookies are usually because the mixture has too much flour in it and not enough egg or liquid.

Cookies will keep for a few days in an airtight tin, but they also freeze very successfully.

carrot and orange cake

The orange juice and zest give this cake a delicious fruity tang, while the nuts and sultanas add lots of texture. You can spread the top of the cake with a little sweetened cream cheese, perhaps flavoured with orange, if it's total indulgence you're after.

SERVES 8–10

125g (4oz) sunflower margarine
125g (4oz) soft brown sugar
2 eggs
2 tbsp clear honey
250g (8oz) self-raising flour
1 tsp baking powder
1 tsp cinnamon
250g (8oz) grated carrot
50g (2oz) walnuts, chopped
50g (2oz) sultanas
zest of 1 orange
50ml (2fl oz) orange juice

1 In a large bowl, cream the fat and sugar until pale and light.

2 Then beat in the eggs and honey.

3 Sift in the flour, baking powder and cinnamon and fold in, then quickly mix in the remaining ingredients.

4 Spoon the mixture into a 23-cm (9-inch) lined and greased cake tin.

5 Bake for 1–1½ hours at 180°C (350°F) Gas Mark 4. Leave in the tin for 10–15 minutes before turning out. Cool on a wire rack.

TIMESAVER *Grate the carrot in a food processor when time is short.*

europe

Having travelled around the world from my kitchen, in a manner of speaking, I've realized how much 'borrowing' of food has been done by intrepid European adventurers and the impact it has had on cookery here.

Europeans over the last few hundred years have been at the centre of travelling and trading and, as a consequence, have imported ideas and ingredients from around the world. Early explorers brought back all manner of foods from their travels, such as the humble potato, colourful tomatoes, highly prized sugar and a wealth of spices. Colonizers from Spain brought back many food items from the New World that we take entirely for granted today such as vanilla, chocolate, the sweet potato and many varieties of beans, courgettes and peppers. Dutch settlers when they returned from Indonesia brought to the Netherlands quite different spices, and British fare with its chutneys has been influenced by the traditions and tastes from different parts of the British Empire.

Ideas and ingredients are almost bound to change as they cross continents and are mixed with local foods or grown in different climates. The Spanish conquistadors, for example, returned from the New World with numerous ingredients including capsicum peppers. The paprika varieties, native to South America, proved adaptable and were able to grow in the cooler climates of Europe. The varieties grown evolved into much milder specimens than their fiery ancestors and the paprika now produced in Spain is valued for its vibrant scarlet colour and subtle flavour rather than its heat.

In more recent times it is not only ingredients that have been acquired, but also techniques such as stir-frying, marinating, roasting and blending of spices. Many Europeans are happy to experiment, but are also fortunate that specialist shops abound and it is therefore easy to create dishes from the Far East or Latin America. From the melting pot of all the indigenous ingredients mixed with the imports, Europe has much to offer.

foods of europe

I've included some great cold-weather foods using the abundance of winter vegetables grown in Europe. The cool climate is just right for producing vegetables of many kinds – onions, potatoes, carrots, beets and leeks – which make marvellous hearty broths and substantial tasty pies, such as the winter vegetable and walnut pie on page 72. Autumn, with its mellow mists at the start and end of the days, is the season for edible mushrooms, many of which are still to be found growing wild in woodlands throughout much of Europe. I've included a smooth full-flavoured mushroom soup with lemon and thyme (*page 50*) to be enjoyed as the nights draw in.

The way vegetables are prepared in the different countries of Europe is extremely varied, with all manner of techniques used, such as grilling, boiling, steaming, sautéing, baking, frying, roasting and griddling. I've included a very simple asparagus dish from Italy as well as a contrasting slow-cooked red cabbage dish from Germany.

There is also in northern Europe a rich tradition of dairy products. It is certainly worth trying the many different cheeses produced by France, Italy, Britain, Ireland and Germany, to name but a few dairy-producing nations. Some of their cheeses are wonderful for cooking, such as the two favourites from Italy, Taleggio, a cow's cheese that melts smoothly and quickly, and mozzarella, made from cow's or buffalo's milk, which I've combined with rice and herbs to make the classic Italian dish of stuffed tomatoes (*page 64*). Creamy goat's cheese with its delicate tang goes wonderfully well with succulent roast vegetables, making a perfect light lunch or starter. Strongly flavoured traditional Cheddar, a splendid versatile cheese, works exceptionally well in tiny delicate soufflés. Look out too for the many regional specialities made from sheep and goat's milk and for handmade cheese to make interesting sandwiches and attractive cheese boards as a perfect end to a meal.

I've also included many dishes featuring the various flavours of the Mediterranean from Spain, France and Italy. These countries are united from a culinary point of view by their copious use of garlic and olive oil and yet there are also quite marked differences in the flavourings that identify these countries' cuisines.

In the south of France, for example, the food is often perfumed with the herbs that abound in the region; typically there are very well-known herbs such as thyme, marjoram, rosemary, basil and bay leaf, with less well-known flavours of fennel, savory and lavender. I am lucky enough to be brought olives from my friend's olive grove on the mountainside near Avignon. These smooth-flavoured olives make a gorgeous tapenade, a rich soft paste made of black olives, garlic, capers, basil, black

or red pepper, which appears on many Provençal hors d'oeuvre tables. It is delicious spread on bread or squares of toast served as finger food. I have made the tapenade into an appetizing tart, mixing it with onions, flavoured with a classic *bouquet garni* (*page 57*).

In Spain, much use is made of tomatoes flavoured with herbs but also, where there was once Moorish influence, there are North African and Oriental spices such as cinnamon, nutmeg, aniseed and cumin seeds. Almonds are a common ingredient introduced by the Moors and they are used for snacks and desserts, as well as for thickening sauces and soups. Ajo Blanco (*page 53*) is a white gazpacho – a chilled soup flavoured with almonds that makes a refreshing summer meal. I've included some delectable and very traditional tapas dishes (*pages 54–55*), as well as *pistou*, a classic Spanish stew (*page 75*) featuring the very common Mediterranean vegetables of aubergines, courgettes and tomatoes, which of course pop up in all guises throughout the region. France and Italy both have quite similar classics in the form of ratatouille, and *caponata*, a delectable dish made using aubergines, capers and olives, from Sicily.

From Italy, where tomatoes, oregano and basil are rarely off the menu, I've included three creamy rich savouries: featherlight pancakes filled with courgettes and ricotta cheese (*pages 62–63*), which are popular in most of Italy (they take a bit of preparation but the end result is worth it). Spinach and ricotta is another mouth-watering combination which I've made into a traditional Easter pie (*pages 70–71*). Tomato sauces are common to all of Italy (there's an easy recipe on *page 49*) and lend themselves to many variations. In the south and in parts of Sicily these sauces are flavoured by mingling sweet and sour ingredients such as olives, raisins, capers and citrus fruits. I love sharp spicy sauces and have included a pine nut and chilli sauce to go with pasta (*page 67*).

To round off your meal there is a gourmet chocolate tart, a positively alcoholic peach dish and a vanilla-flavoured apple cake (*pages 78–81*).

common ingredients and useful techniques

basil

Basil thrives in warm climates and is used extensively in Mediterranean cookery. It goes brilliantly with tomatoes and is excellent in salad dressings. It is best used raw, but if added to hot dishes, do this just before serving, as basil quickly loses its flavour.

bay leaf

This evergreen tree with aromatic leaves is native to the Mediterranean. Once dried, the leaves turn a pale greyish green colour. Bay leaves can be used to flavour most savoury dishes as well as giving a slight almond flavour to cream and custards. Remember always to remove the bay leaf before serving.

caper

Caper berries are tiny buds with a piquant flavour. They go well with garlic and lemon and act as a good foil for an oily dish such as roasted vegetables.

oregano

Commonly used in Italian and Greek dishes, oregano works particularly well with basil and adds a strong flavour to cheese dishes and tomato-based sauces.

parsley

Parsley enhances the taste of other herbs. There are two types with similar flavours: flat-leaf, which resembles coriander, and curly-leaf. Use parsley for herb butters or mixing with soft cheese, sprinkle onto pasta and potatoes, and use in egg dishes and sauces.

pine nuts

These slim oval seeds have a distinctive if subtle flavour. They are great lightly toasted in salads, with roasted vegetables, and go well with Mediterranean ingredients, particularly tomatoes and peppers. Ground with basil, parmesan and olive oil they make the classic sauce, pesto.

root vegetables

These vegetables are used widely in Europe, especially in cold-weather casseroles and stews. They make smooth purées, which can be enriched with cream or soft cheese, and are delicious roasted, which brings out their natural sweet, mellow flavour. Carrots and potatoes are familiar roots, but look out for the less well-known swede, turnip, parsnip, kohlrabi, celeriac and Jerusalem artichoke. Buy vegetables that feel firm and heavy. Kept in cool, well-ventilated conditions, they should last several weeks.

making classic herb mixtures

bouquet garni

A bouquet garni is made by tying together bay leaf, thyme, parsley and rosemary. It is good for flavouring slow cooking dishes.

fines herbes

Using equal quantities of chives, chervil, parsley and tarragon makes a great flavouring for egg dishes, such as soufflés, omelettes and quiches

herbes de provence

Herbes de Provence is a mixture of thyme, rosemary, bay, basil and savory (occasionally lavender) and as you would expect works well with vegetables from the Mediterranean.

white sauce

MAKES 300ML (10FL OZ)

300ml (10fl oz) milk
1/2 onion
1 bay leaf
6 black peppercorns
1 sprig of thyme
generous grating of nutmeg
25g (1oz) butter
25g (1oz) flour
salt and pepper

1 Heat the milk with the onion, bay leaf, peppercorns, thyme and nutmeg until just warm and then leave for 15 minutes. Strain through a sieve.

2 Melt the butter in a small pan and when it is foaming sprinkle over the flour. Mix well and cook over a gentle heat for 2–3 minutes.

3 Add the milk a quarter at a time stirring very well.

4 Bring the sauce to boiling point stirring constantly and then simmer over a very gentle heat for 3–4 minutes.

5 Season well and use as required.

tomato sauce

MAKES 500ML (15FL OZ)

2 tbsp olive oil
1 onion, finely chopped
2 x 400g (14oz) cans chopped tomatoes
1 tsp sugar
1 tsp salt
1 bay leaf
1 tsp dried thyme or oregano
pepper

1 Heat the oil in a large pan and gently fry the onions until translucent. Make sure the onion is really soft before adding other ingredients.

2 Add the tomatoes, sugar, salt, bay leaf and thyme. Bring to the boil, reduce the heat, cover and cook slowly for 30 minutes. Leave to cool slightly, then using a food processor or blender, blend the tomato mixture until it is very smooth. Adjust the seasoning and use as required.

mushroom soup with lemon and thyme

soupe de champignons au citron et thym

Mushrooms do have a wonderful flavour, adding richness and depth to soups, stews and sauces and can add an intensity to stocks. Using dried mushrooms is an easy way of achieving this. Dried wild mushrooms at first glance seem wildly expensive but remember that you only need small quantities as they should reconstitute to about 4 or 5 times their original weight.

SERVES 4

25g (1oz) dried ceps
450ml (15fl oz) boiling water
1 tbsp butter
1 onion, finely chopped
2 sticks celery, finely diced
50g (2oz) potato, peeled and diced
150g (5oz) mushrooms, finely diced
300ml (10fl oz) vegetable stock
1 tsp dried thyme
4 tbsp double cream
1 tbsp lemon juice
salt and pepper

1 Infuse the ceps in the boiling water for 15 minutes.

2 In a large pan melt the butter and gently sweat the onion for about 5 minutes. Add the celery and cook for 5 minutes. Add the potato and cook for 2–3 minutes. Finally, add the mushrooms and cook for 2–3 minutes.

3 Pour on the infused water, chopping the ceps finely if necessary. Add the stock.

4 Bring to the boil and add the thyme, then simmer covered for 30 minutes or until the potato is very soft.

5 Leave to cool, then process in a food processor until smooth. Add the cream and lemon and season to taste.

6 Reheat gently before serving.

white gazpacho

ajo blanco

This smooth, white refreshing Spanish soup is best appreciated on a hot summer evening. The delicate almond flavour is wonderfully balanced by the tang of garlic and vinegar and the sweetness of the grapes. Make sure it is well chilled. My Spanish friends tell me that if they are in a hurry, they use chilled water and sometimes process in some ice cubes as a short cut. Use whole almonds rather than ready-ground as they have a much better flavour.

SERVES 6

150g (5oz) white bread
1 litre (1¾ pints) water
250g (8oz) whole blanched almonds
3 cloves garlic, crushed
125ml (4fl oz) olive oil
1–2 tbsp white wine vinegar
salt
200g (7oz) green grapes, halved.

1 Soak the bread in about 100ml (3½fl oz) water. This makes the almond mixture easier to process.

2 Put the almonds, crushed garlic, soaked bread and water in a blender or a food processor. Blend until smooth, then add a tablespoon of oil a little at a time, then a teaspoon of vinegar and then the remaining oil, pouring it on in a thin stream while the blender is still running. Then add the remaining vinegar to taste and season. Chill well.

3 Just before serving add the grapes. Float them in the soup cut sides uppermost otherwise they will sink to the bottom of the bowl very rapidly.

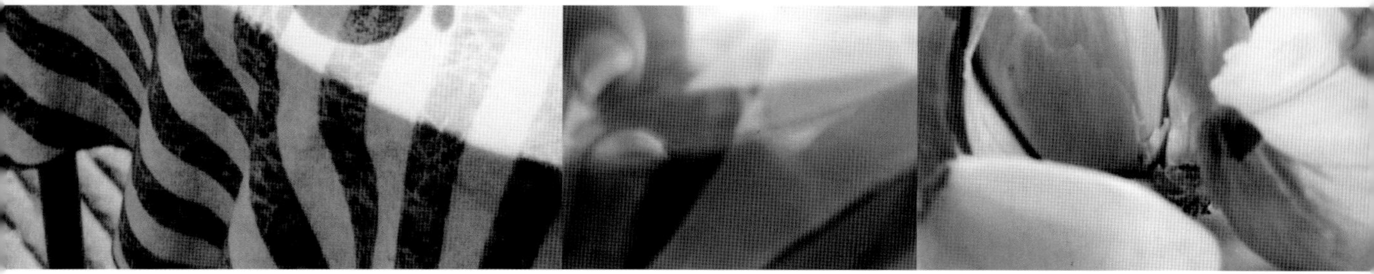

tapas

An array of tapas is served with drinks in virtually every Spanish bar, and would likely include olives, roasted vegetables, simple dips, small cheese-filled pastries or slices of Spanish-style omelette. The recipes here are traditional favourites.

vegetable and potato salad

ensalada russe

4 medium potatoes, peeled, boiled and diced
2 carrots, boiled and diced
125g (4oz) cooked peas
2 tbsp olive oil
2 tbsp red wine vinegar
pinch of sugar
150g (5oz) mayonnaise
1 clove garlic, crushed
salt and pepper
1 red pepper, to garnish

1 Prepare and cook the potatoes, carrots and peas and set them to one side.

2 In a small bowl, mix together the oil, vinegar and sugar. Then season to taste and pour this mixture over the freshly cooked vegetables. Chill for 2 hours.

3 Mix the mayonnaise with the garlic and then mix this into the vegetables. Adjust seasoning.

4 Chill again.

5 For the garnish, grill the pepper until the skin is evenly charred, then remove the skin and cut into thin strips. Arrange over the salad before serving.

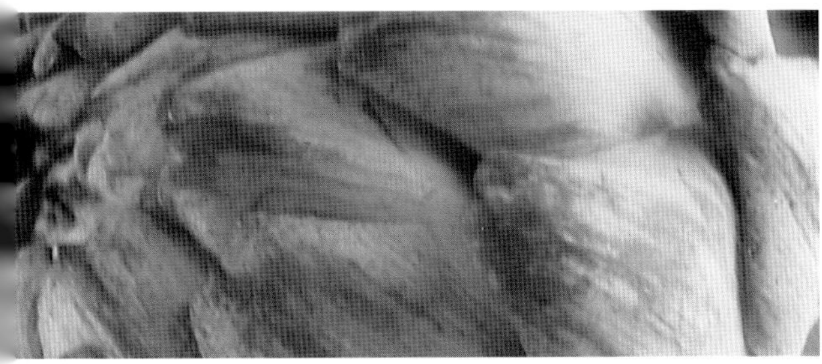

andalucian bean salad

habas al andalucia

1 tbsp olive oil
2 tbsp chopped onion
2 cloves garlic, chopped
2 tomatoes, chopped
400g (14oz) (net weight) canned cannellini or lima beans, rinsed and dried
4–6 artichoke hearts, halved
175ml (6fl oz) vegetable stock or water
1 bay leaf
pinch of saffron
½ tsp ground cumin
juice of ½ lemon
2 tbsp chopped parsley
salt and pepper

1 Heat the oil in a medium pan and cook the onion and garlic until soft, then add the tomatoes and cook for 4–5 minutes.

2 Stir in the remaining ingredients except the parsley and bring to the boil, then simmer gently for about 10 minutes for the flavours to develop.

3 Season to taste, add the lemon juice and lightly mix in the parsley.

mushrooms in sherry

champiñones al jerez

450g (1lb) button mushrooms
3–4 tbsp lemon juice
2 tbsp olive oil
2 tbsp onion, chopped
½–1 tsp plain flour
50ml (2fl oz) sherry
50ml (2fl oz) vegetable stock
2 tbsp chopped parsley
salt and pepper

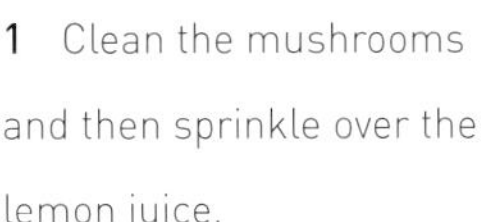

1 Clean the mushrooms and then sprinkle over the lemon juice.

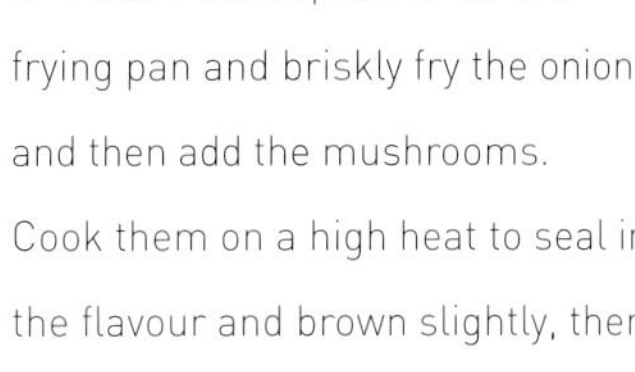

2 Heat 1 tablespoon of oil in a frying pan and briskly fry the onion and then add the mushrooms. Cook them on a high heat to seal in the flavour and brown slightly, then transfer everything to a warm plate.

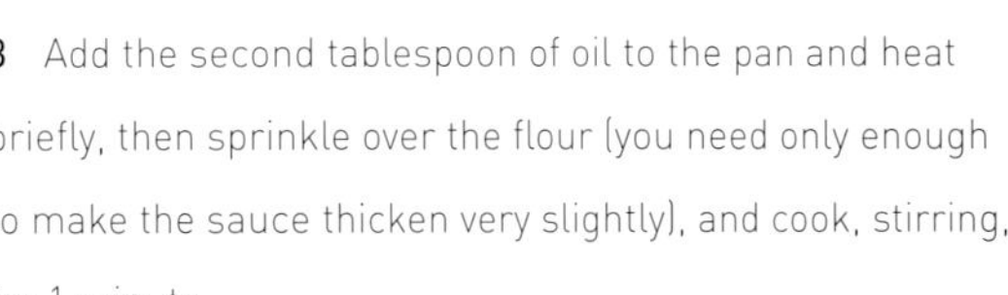

3 Add the second tablespoon of oil to the pan and heat briefly, then sprinkle over the flour (you need only enough to make the sauce thicken very slightly), and cook, stirring, for 1 minute.

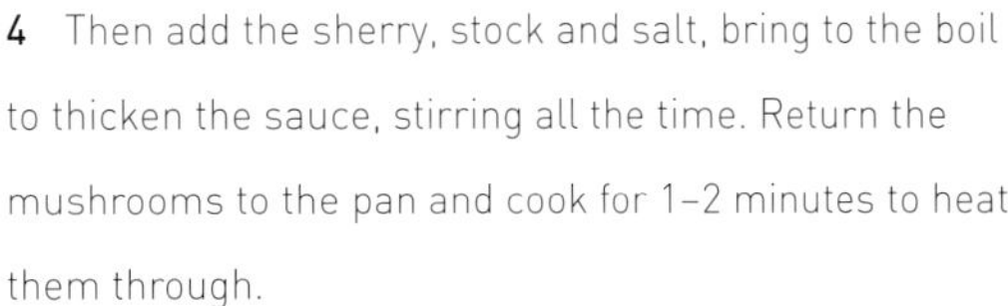

4 Then add the sherry, stock and salt, bring to the boil to thicken the sauce, stirring all the time. Return the mushrooms to the pan and cook for 1–2 minutes to heat them through.

5 Adjust the seasoning and serve hot, garnished with chopped parsley.

onion tart with tapenade

pissaladière au tapenade

This is a cross between a flan and pizza with a crisp base and vegetable topping. The tapenade, a powerful olive paste (see pages 46–47) makes a marvellous flavour base.

SERVES 6–8

FOR THE PASTRY

200g (7oz) plain flour
pinch of salt
100g ($3\frac{1}{2}$oz) butter
3–4 tbsp chilled water

FOR THE FILLING

4 tbsp olive oil
900g (2lb) onions, chopped
2 garlic cloves, crushed
1 bouquet garni (*see page 49*)
2–3 tbsp tapenade
2 leeks, white parts only, cut into rounds
12 black olives
salt and pepper

1 To make the pastry, sift the flour and salt into a large bowl then rub in the butter until the mixture resembles fine breadcrumbs. Add the water gradually and draw the mixture to a dough. Knead very lightly and then wrap in clingfilm and chill for 30 minutes.

2 On a lightly floured surface, roll out the dough to fit on a Swiss roll tin. Prick the base all over and line with greaseproof paper, then fill the shell with dried beans or ceramic baking beans.

3 Bake at 200°C (400°F) Gas Mark 6 for 10 minutes, then remove the beans and greaseproof paper and bake for a further 10 minutes or until the pastry is golden and crisp.

4 For the filling, heat the oil and add the onions, garlic and bouquet garni and cook for about 10 minutes until the onions are soft. Add 2–3 tablespoons of water and a little salt. Continue to stew the onions until really soft. Remove the bouquet garni and leave to cool.

5 Mix the cooled onions with the tapenade and spread thickly over the pastry. Arrange the leeks on top and dot with a few olives. Brush everything with olive oil.

6 Bake for 10 minutes at 200°C (400°F) Gas Mark 6. Serve warm, or at room temperature, as a starter or light lunch.

goat's cheese roulé with roasted peppers

roulé de fromage de chèvre au poivron grillé

For this colourful, flavoursome dish, choose a fairly firm goat's cheese with a clean tangy taste. You need to be able to mash it with the other ingredients before leaving it to set. This is a great recipe for entertaining as so much can be prepared well ahead of time.

SERVES 4–6

FOR THE ROULÉ

150g (5oz) goat's cheese, fairly firm texture
50g (2oz) butter, softened
3½ tbsp double cream
25g (1oz) Parmesan cheese, freshly grated
2 tbsp finely chopped parsley
1 tsp lemon zest
1 clove garlic, crushed
pinch of cayenne
salt and pepper

2 red peppers
2 yellow peppers
2 tbsp olive oil
8 cloves garlic
½ tsp chilli flakes
12 black olives, chopped
1 tbsp capers, chopped
1 tbsp lemon juice

1 In a large bowl, mash the cheese with the softened butter, cream and Parmesan, parsley, lemon zest, garlic and cayenne. Season well with pepper and salt to taste. Shape into a round log (roulé) about 2.5-cm (1-inch) in diameter, wrap in clingfilm and chill for 1 hour or until firm.

2 Halve the peppers and remove the seeds and white membrane. Brush the outer skins with olive oil. Put a whole clove of garlic in each pepper half, add a sprinkling of red chilli flakes and place on a small baking tray. Bake for 35–40 minutes at 200°C (400°F) Gas Mark 6.

3 Leave to cool slightly then peel off the pepper skins and let cool completely in the cooking juices.

4 Remove the cloves of garlic and squeeze the flesh out of the skin. Cut the peppers into thick slices. Toss the chopped olives and capers into the cooking liquor and add the roasted garlic flesh plus lemon juice to taste. Season well.

5 Slice the roulé and serve with the roasted pepper strips, sprinkled with the chopped olives, capers and roasted garlic.

watercress and cheddar soufflé

Light delicate soufflés still have an air of mystery to them – how did anyone discover the properties of whisked egg whites? These individual soufflés are easy and quick to make. You can get the mixture ready and leave beating the egg whites until ready to cook.

SERVES 4

100g (3½oz) watercress (or 50g (2oz) watercress and 50g (2oz) rocket)
25g (1oz) butter
25g (1oz) plain flour
125ml (4fl oz) milk
100g (3½oz) grated Cheddar cheese
2 eggs

1 Cover the watercress or watercress and rocket with boiling water, leave for 30 seconds and then drain. Squeeze dry and chop very finely.

2 Lightly grease 4 ramekin dishes.

3 Melt the butter and stir in the flour and cook the roux for 1 minute. Then add the milk and stirring constantly bring the sauce to the boil and simmer for 2–3 minutes. It should be very thick. Season well and add the cheese.

4 Separate the eggs. Mix the yolks into the cheese sauce.

5 In a large bowl whisk the egg whites until stiff. Stir 1 tablespoon of the egg white into the cheese sauce. Then fold in the remaining egg white using a metal spoon.

6 Spoon the mixture into the prepared ramekins.

7 Bake at 200°C (400°F) Gas Mark 6 for 15 minutes. Serve immediately.

courgette and ricotta crêpes

crepes con ricotta e zucchini

Crêpes and pancakes appear in many guises in northern Europe, France and throughout Italy. In Britain they are generally served as a sweet dish with lemon and sugar. In France, crêpes were originally called galettes crêpes, meaning flat cakes. Crêpes originated in Brittany, the north-west region of France, where they rarely had fillings and were used as bread. Until about a 100 years ago, all crêpes were made of buckwheat flour after the Crusaders brought back buckwheat from the Middle East. Buckwheat tends to make the batter denser but it gives a wonderful flavour, In this recipe you can use all wheat flour or try adding a little buckwheat to the mix.

SERVES 4–6

FOR THE CRÊPES

2 eggs
300ml (10fl oz) milk
100g (3½oz) plain flour

FOR THE FILLING

2 tbsp olive oil
3 medium courgettes, grated
2 cloves garlic, crushed
25g (1oz) butter
25g (1oz) plain flour
300ml (10fl oz) milk, warmed with ½ onion, bay leaf and grating of nutmeg
2 tsp oregano
200g (7oz) ricotta cheese
50g (2oz) Parmesan cheese
300ml (10fl oz) vegetable stock
1 tbsp butter for greasing the dish

1 To make the crêpes, put the milk and eggs into a blender and process for 30 seconds, then add the flour and process again for up to 1 minute or until the batter is smooth and thick. Leave to stand for 30 minutes.

2 Heat a little butter or drizzle of oil in a crêpe pan and fry 2 tablespoons of the mixture for 1 minute on either side to make a crêpe. Repeat until you have made 8 medium or 12 small crepes. Set aside.

3 To make the filling, heat the oil in a frying pan and fry the courgettes with the garlic on a medium heat, stirring well until the courgettes are golden brown.

4 Pat off excess oil with kitchen paper.

5 Make a béchamel sauce by melting the butter in a small pan and then stirring in the flour. Cook over a low heat for 1 minute then pour on at least ⅓ of the warm milk, stir well until the mixture is smooth, then add the remaining milk stirring constantly until the sauce is smooth, bring to the boil and simmer for 2–3 minutes. Season to taste.

6 Mix the courgettes and ricotta into the sauce with half the Parmesan. Adjust the seasoning.

7 Spoon filling into each crêpe and place the filled crêpes in one layer in a well buttered ovenproof dish.

8 Pour over the stock and sprinkle on the remaining Parmesan.

9 Bake for 12–15 minutes 190°C (375°F) Gas Mark 5. Serve hot.

tomatoes stuffed with rice and herbs

pomodori ripieni

This easy Italian dish makes a light and colourful supper. Choose really large well-flavoured tomatoes and very fresh herbs. If you are a garlic lover, adding a clove of garlic into the boiled rice gives extra zip to the filling.

SERVES 4

4 large Italian tomatoes
100g (3½oz) long grain rice
100g (3½oz) mozzarella, cubed
6 tbsp fresh basil, chopped
4 tbsp fresh mint, chopped
2 tbsp olive oil
salt
fresh basil leaves, to garnish

1 Cut the tops off the tomatoes and set aside. Scoop out the flesh, chop and set aside. Salt the inside of the tomatoes and place upside down to drain.

2 Meanwhile, boil the rice for about 20 minutes or until tender in lightly salted water, drain and sprinkle over some cold water to stop cooking.

3 Mix the cooked rice with the chopped tomato, mozzarella, basil and mint, 1 tablespoon olive oil and salt to taste.

4 Stuff the tomatoes with the mixture, put their tops back on and place in a lightly oiled ovenproof dish, drizzle over a little more oil and bake at 180°C (350°F) Gas Mark 4 for about half an hour.

5 Serve warm or cold.

6 Garnish with extra basil leaves.

tagliatelle with pine nut and chilli sauce

tagliatelle con pinoli e peperoncino rosso

Sweet and hot flavours combined in a rich tomato sauce are popular throughout southern Italy and Sicily. Cook the broccoli until only just tender so that it is still bright and fresh when stirred into the sauce.

SERVES 4

1 tbsp olive oil
2 shallots, finely chopped
1 clove garlic, crushed
½ tsp dried chilli flakes
25g (1oz) pine nuts
4 tbsp red wine
1 x 400g (14oz) can chopped tomatoes
400–500g (14–16oz) tagliatelle
250g (8oz) florets broccoli
50g (2oz) raisins
salt and pepper
4 tbsp freshly grated Parmesan cheese

1 Heat the oil in a pan and gently fry the shallot, garlic, chilli flakes and pine nuts until the shallots are translucent and the pine nuts lightly toasted.

2 Add the red wine and cook over a medium heat stirring briskly until the liquid has evaporated.

3 Add the tomatoes and bring the sauce to the boil, then cover and simmer for 25 minutes.

4 When the sauce is ready, cook the pasta in a large pan of boiling salted water. Once the pasta is boiling, in a separate pan, steam the broccoli and raisins for 5–7 minutes until the raisins are plum and the broccoli tender.

5 Toss the cooked broccoli and raisins into the sauce and cook for 1 minute to heat through. Drain the pasta and serve on warm plates with the sauce spooned over the top and Parmesan cheese on the side.

pastry

Europe certainly has no monopoly on pastry, though possibly the first pastry recipe – a delicious-sounding concoction of goat's cheese and honey with a rye flour crust – came from Rome. In Europe, the reliance on wheat, and a cool climate for much of the year in some regions, means that wheat-based pastry features in many classic dishes such as quiche from France, or English pies, as well as filo pastry.

Pastry making is a skill but, as with many other processes in cooking, practice, knowing how and why, and following some simple rules can make the end results much better and more successful.

There are many types of pastry that can be used for sweet and savoury recipes. Plain shortcrust is good for tart and quiche bases; richer shortcrust pastry is good for fruit pies, particularly ones that are to be eaten cold; rough puff is good for little pies and pasties; and finally, filo pastry is good for layered savouries as well as individually wrapped parcels.

When making pastry it is best to work in a cool room with cool or chilled ingredients, particularly any fat used and water for binding. Handle pastry lightly but firmly. Wet pastry will be tough and hard once baked. Dry pastry is difficult to roll out as it cracks or crumbles. All pastry benefits from resting in the refrigerator before being rolled out as this prevents it shrinking during baking.

shortcrust

Unlike classic shortcrust, this has more fat, sugar to improve elasticity, and baking powder to make it light.

250g (8oz) plain flour
pinch salt
$^1/_2$ tsp baking powder
125g (4oz) chilled butter, vegetable fat or a mixture
1 tsp caster sugar
1 tbsp sunflower oil
4–6 tbsp cold water

1 Mix the flour, salt, sugar and baking powder in a large bowl. Cut in the fat and rub in until the mixture resembles fine bread crumbs. Shake the bowl occasionally so that the

larger lumps rise to the top. If using a blender or food processor, process in short bursts to ensure the fat and flour are not over processed.

2 Add the oil and water and mix to a dough. Knead lightly and wrap in clingfilm and chill for 30 minutes. Use as required.

quick flaky pastry

Do remember to have chilled water ready and the fat frozen so that it is very easy to grate.

Makes approximately 550g (1lb/4oz) dough

250g (8oz) plain flour
1/2 tsp salt
150g (5oz) solid vegetable fat and/or butter, frozen for 30 minutes prior to using
1 tbsp lemon juice
125–150ml (4–5fl oz) ice-cold water
1 egg yolk

1 Mix the flour with the salt in a large bowl.

2 Grate in the frozen fat or mixture of fats.

3 Add the lemon juice and just enough water to make a dough. Draw up to a ball and knead very lightly.

4 Wrap the dough in clingfilm and chill for 30 minutes. Roll out dough to a long oblong, fold in bottom third, then top third. Seal the edges and make a quarter turn. Repeat this and chill again for 30 minutes.

filo pastry

Ready-made filo pastry makes light paper thin layers for enclosing savoury and sweet filling and for making single triangles and mini strudels. It dries out very quickly so have any filling prepared in advance, and cover the sheets you are not using with a damp tea towel or cloth. Each sheet needs to be liberally brushed with either melted butter, oil (olive, sunflower or vegetable) or a mixture of the two.

baking blind

This refers to baking a pastry case before it is filled.The base should be pricked with a fork, covered with greaseproof paper and weighted down with dried beans or rice or ceramic baking beans. Cook in a hot oven until set, remove the beans and paper, and cook further to crisp.

easter pie

torta pasqualina

This is an Easter dish from Italy, at one time made for the holiday after Easter but now variations appear at other times of the year. Traditionally whole eggs are cooked into this pie by breaking them into indentations made in the spinach and ricotta mixture. You can use large or medium eggs. If you use large ones, you may find there is too much egg white, in that case roughly separate the eggs and put the yolks with a little egg white into the indentations in the pie. If you are in a hurry, you can simply mix the eggs in with the spinach and ricotta mixture.

SERVES 6

500g (1lb 2oz) spinach
25g (1oz) butter
1 onion, finely chopped
2 cloves garlic, finely chopped
500g (1lb 2oz) ricotta cheese
4 eggs
100g (4oz) Parmesan cheese
¼ tsp nutmeg
salt and pepper
for the pastry
6–8 tbsp olive oil
12 sheets filo pastry

1 Wash the spinach and cook it for 4–5 minutes in a covered pan. Drain, squeeze dry and chop finely.

2 Melt the butter in a large pan and cook the onion and garlic over a gentle heat until translucent. Add the spinach and cook for 2 minutes. Leave to cool. Beat the ricotta and mix it thoroughly into the spinach with 50g (2oz) Parmesan and season very well with the nutmeg, salt and pepper. (At this stage beat in the eggs if you wish).

3 To assemble the pie, brush the olive oil over the base of a square ovenproof dish.

4 Brush the olive oil over one sheet of filo and line the base and sides of the dish

5 Then place another sheet of filo on top and brush with more oil. Continue until you have a base of 6 sheets.

6 Put the spinach and ricotta mixture on top and make 4 indentations.

7 Break the eggs into a little bowl one at a time and then slide them into the holes. Season each egg and sprinkle over the remaining Parmesan.

8 Cover the mixture with a sheet of filo brushed with oil and tuck in the edges. Do not press down. Repeat this using the remaining sheets.

9 Mark a cross through the centre of the pastry with a sharp knife.

10 Bake at 200°C (400°F) Gas Mark 6 for 34–40 minutes or until the pastry is crisp and golden. Turn the oven down a little for the last 10 minutes if the pastry is becoming too brown. Serve hot.

winter vegetable and walnut pie

A plethora of root vegetables such as parsnip, celeriac, turnip and swede herald in the autumn in northern Europe. These vegetables are a boon to soups, stews and pies as they add substance, colour and flavour and provide heart-warming meals.

SERVES 4

450g (1lb) potatoes, peeled and chopped
400g (14oz) celeriac, peeled and chopped
50g (2oz) butter
50g (2oz) Puy lentils
2 shallots, diced
200g (7oz) leeks, cleaned and sliced
200g (7oz) parsnip, peeled and diced
75g (3oz) walnut pieces
½ tsp dried herbs (thyme, marjoram or oregano)
400g (14oz) can tomatoes, chopped
100g (3½oz) grated Cheddar cheese
salt and pepper

1 Boil the potatoes and celeriac together in a large pan of boiling, lightly salted water. Once cooked, drain and mash with 25g (1oz) butter.

2 Cook the lentils in a pan of boiling water until soft. The quick-cooking varieties should only take 10–15 minutes. Drain and set aside.

3 Heat the remaining 25g (1oz) butter and sweat the shallots, leeks and parsnips over a low heat for about 10 minutes, stir in the walnuts and add the herbs, cooked lentils and tomatoes. Mix well and season to taste.

4 Spoon the vegetable mixture into a deep ovenproof dish and cover with the mashed potato and celeriac. Sprinkle over the grated cheese and bake at 180°C (350°F) Gas Mark 4 for 30–35 minutes. Serve hot.

pistou with eggs

pistou con huevos

Pistou is a Spanish-style stew using summer vegetables from the Mediterranean, namely courgettes, peppers and aubergines. It is quick and easy to make but for the best results cook it slowly so that the flavour of the vegetables permeates through the stew. At the end of cooking, break in an egg and bake in the oven. It is a great combination served with crusty bread and salad.

SERVES 4

2 courgettes
1 green pepper
1 red pepper
1 aubergine
1 onion chopped
3 tbsp olive oil
400g (14oz) can chopped tomatoes
2 tbsp parsley, chopped
4 eggs
salt and pepper

1 Cut the courgettes, peppers and aubergine into small cubes.

2 Heat the olive oil in a large pan and cook the onion slowly for 4–5 minutes.

3 Then add the vegetables, mix everything together, and cook very slowly over a medium to low heat. This takes 30–45 minutes.

4 Add the canned tomatoes, parsely and seasoning and cook for a further 15 minutes.

5 Spoon the hot pistou into small ovenproof bowls.

6 Break an egg into each bowl and bake at 180°C (350°F) Gas Mark 4 for 12–15 minutes until the egg is cooked.

asparagus with taleggio and parmesan

This delicious simple asparagus dish can be served as a starter or a side dish. Taleggio is a soft creamy cheese with a rich buttery flavour and slight saltiness. It melts beautifully which makes it ideal for gratin dishes. A similar cheese from the same family is Bel Paese.

SERVES 4

450g (1lb) asparagus
125g (4oz) taleggio cheese
25g (1oz) freshly grated Parmesan cheese
25g (1oz) butter
salt and pepper

1 Trim off the tough ends of the asparagus.

2 Steam the asparagus for 2–3 minutes or until just tender. The asparagus could also be microwaved until just cooked. The length of time this takes will vary according to the power setting on the microwave.

3 Grease a baking dish with butter and lay half the asparagus in the dish, placing all the tips the same way. Cover with half the taleggio cut in rough slices and a sprinkling of Parmesan and season with salt and pepper.

4 Place a second row on top with the tips placed at right angles to the bottom row, then cover with the remainder of the cheeses and season well.

5 Bake the asparagus at 200°C (400°F) Gas Mark 6 for 5–10 minutes until the cheese has just melted. Serve hot.

red cabbage with apple and cloves

rotkohl

Red cabbage is a splendid vegetable; good value, wonderful taste and flavour, and can be cooked in many different ways. I have suggested a spiced mixture with apple and onion and cloves but you can use nutmeg, ginger or caraway as well as sultanas, oranges, apricots and beetroots. It's fine to make huge quantities because when cooked it freezes well but can be quickly defrosted. Look out for baby red cabbage which can be used for just one meal.

SERVES 4–6

450g (1lb) red cabbage
1 tbsp sunflower oil
1 large onion, chopped
2 dessert apples, peeled and grated
3–4 cloves
1 tsp cinnamon
1 tsp sugar
2 tbsp red wine vinegar or cider vinegar
salt

1 Shred the cabbage finely, either by hand or using the slicing blade on a food processor.

2 In a large pan heat the oil and fry the onion until just soft.

3 Add the cabbage and apple and mix in well, then add the remaining ingredients.

4 Cover the pan and simmer the mixture for 35–40 minutes until the cabbage is really soft. Alternatively, place the mixture in an ovenproof dish and bake for 45–60 minutes at 190°C (375°F) Gas Mark 5 or until the cabbage is very soft.

5 Adjust the seasoning and serve hot or cold.

chocolate and pear tart

tarte aux poires et chocolat

This is a rich tart which uses the classic combination of chocolate and pears. Be sure you have ripe pears so, if necessary, buy them a few days in advance.

SERVES 8–10

200g (7oz) plain flour
2 tbsp caster sugar
pinch of salt
100g (3½oz) unsalted butter, diced
1 egg, lightly beaten
2 tsp water

FOR THE FILLING
200g (7oz) dark chocolate
125g (4oz) unsalted butter
3 eggs
4 tbsp caster sugar
2 large or 3 small ripe pears

1 For the pastry, in a large bowl mix the flour with the sugar and a pinch of salt. Using your fingertips, rub in the butter until the mixture resembles fine breadcrumbs. If using a food processor, process the mixture in short bursts until you achieve the right consistency.

2 Add the egg and work the mixture with a palette knife or pastry scraper adding the water 1 teaspoon at a time until the dough begins to hold together. Bring the dough together with your hands and shape into a rough ball.

3 Wrap in clingfilm and chill for 30 minutes.

4 Leave the dough for a few minutes after taking it out of the fridge, then roll it evenly to fill a 23-cm (9-inch) flan dish and chill for 30 minutes.

5 Bake blind for 15 minutes at 180°C (350°F) Gas Mark 4 (*see page 69* for details). Remove beans and parchment and bake for a further 10 minutes.

6 To make the filling, melt the chocolate and butter in the microwave. This takes 2 minutes at 600W but the time will vary according to your microwave. Alternatively, melt the chocolate and butter in a bowl over a pan of hot water.

7 Whisk the eggs and sugar for about 4–5 minutes over a bowl of hot water until double the volume. Fold into the chocolate and butter mixture and pour the mixture into the prepared pastry case.

8 Peel and quarter the pears and arrange in the chocolate mixture. Bake for 12–15 minutes at 180°C (350°F) Gas Mark 4 until just set. Leave to cool in the dish then chill well. Remove from the refrigerator 10 minutes before serving.

COOK'S TIP *Pears go brown as they cook, so brush them with a little apricot glaze once the tart is cooked.*

peaches in amaretto

peschi all'amaretto

This recipe comes from a guest house on the shores of Lake Garda, though it is well known in many parts of Italy. It is a fabulous way to cook peaches and other soft stone fruit. Serve them warm, with the sauce spooned over, with vanilla ice cream. Amaretti are tiny brittle almond macaroons; Amaretto is a liqueur made from apricot kernels which has a pronounced almond flavour.

SERVES 4

- 4 ripe peaches
- 75–100g (3–½oz) amaretti, coarsely crumbled
- 7 tbsp marsala or Amaretto di Saranno
- 7 tbsp sweet red wine
- 2–3 tbsp unsalted butter

1 Butter an ovenproof dish with unsalted butter.

2 Wash and halve the peaches, removing the stones without damaging the shape of the peaches. In a bowl, mix the amaretti with the marsala or Amaretto. (Leaving the amaretti quite coarse will give a crunchy texture to the finished dish.)

3 Spoon this mixture into the hollow of each peach half, then spoon some more onto the cut edge. Drizzle with red wine, some of which will go onto the oven dish. Divide the butter between the 8 peach halves dotting it on the cut surfaces rather than the crumb mixture as that tends to absorb the butter and you will get less sauce. Bake for about 20 minutes at 180°C (350°F) Gas Mark 4, basting once or twice.

Annette's apple cake

apfelkuchen

I lived for a year in Berlin sampling the many delights of German baking with my morning coffee. Apple cakes remain my favourite. In this version, there is a covering of ground almonds and vanilla which is quite delicious!

SERVES 6

200g (7oz) butter
100g (3½oz) caster sugar
4 eggs, at room temperature
200g (7oz) plain flour
2 tsp baking powder
2 tsp fresh lemon juice
3–4 dessert apples, peeled, cored and quartered
75g (3oz) chopped almonds
1 tsp ground cinnamon
2 tsp vanilla sugar

1 Grease a 23-cm (9-inch) round deep cake tin.

2 In a large bowl, cream the butter and sugar until light. Add the eggs one at a time beating well, add a spoonful of flour if the mixture starts to curdle when adding the eggs. Then sift in the flour and baking powder. (Alternatively, simply put the butter, sugar, sifted flour, eggs and baking powder in a large bowl and mix with an electric mixer for 2 minutes.) Mix together adding the lemon juice. Spoon into prepared pan.

3 Use a small knife to make deep lengthways cuts in the back of each apple quarter. Then place the quarters into the dough, cut sides uppermost.

4 Combine the almonds, ground cinnamon and vanilla sugar and sprinkle on top of the apples.

5 Bake for 50–55 minutes at 180°C (350°F) Gas Mark 4. Leave in the tin for 10–15 minutes before turning out. Cool on a wire rack.

middle east lebanon, turkey, greece

I love the food from these regions and thoroughly enjoyed tasting all the recipes I was shown. As well as tasting, I was busy scribbling notes to catch up on all the asides on the recipes: 'well, we do it like this in our family, but in the south it's made in a different way', 'you can just serve this plain, but we prefer it sprinkled with sumac', and so on. So many variations. What impressed me most was the speed at which dishes were created, mainly because they comprised a few ingredients that work well together, used one pot for cooking and bold seasoning.

Broadly speaking, the food is characterized by an abundance of both herbs and spices, along with widespread use of olive oil and lemons. The Middle Eastern diet embodies many of today's healthy eating principles, namely plenty of fresh vegetables and fruit, wholesome pulses and grains and few animal fats.

Working with and learning from Greek, Lebanese and Turkish cooks, I saw the similarities in cooking methods and styles. Olive oil, for example, is widely used to marinate and infuse flavours, as in Turkish *zeytinyagli* or Lebanese *b'zeit*. There are many versions of classics dishes such as *tabbouleh* and *fattouch* with subtle changes in the balance of the ingredients or use of seasoning such as sumac. Stuffed vegetables, savoury pastries and flat breads are typical of each country, though they may be prepared or seasoned differently. I have included a flavourful stuffing for vine leaves (*page 97*) which was all the more interesting for me as the rice used in the filling is raw.

There is a strong tradition of handing down recipes through families. I was shown many Lebanese recipes by the mother of a friend, who, when she introduced me, stayed to watch her mother cook and to listen to all the stories behind the recipes. The mother explained the lack of garlic in some of the recipes she was showing me, as she had adapted them to suit her daughter's taste. Meanwhile my friend explained that she was busy adding garlic back to recipes as her own daughter had said she preferred the food at her grandmother's house!

lebanon

Lebanese cuisine includes a wealth of simple, tasty vegetarian food which has the added benefit of being easy to prepare. The staples are bulgur wheat and rice, an abundance of fresh vegetables such as peppers, aubergines and green beans, and lavish use of garlic and olive oil. Vegetables are eaten cooked, raw or – when served with pulses (see the recipe for *moujadara, page 100*) – pickled. Flavourings in many recipes are bold, with a focus on fresh herbs such as mint, coriander and parsley, as the dense green herb and bulgur-wheat salad *tabbouleh* exemplifies. Spices are aromatic rather than explosive with frequent use of cumin, coriander and caraway. One spice I had barely tasted before was sumac, a dark red berry with a tart lemony taste which cuts through oily or earthy flavours. It is sold as dry berries or crushed, but you'll find the crushed form more useful.

Pulses feature in many recipes – from small lentils which cook down to a purée and readily absorb flavours to whole beans, commonly served in the *b'zeit* style (with olive oil, which adds a luscious quality) – and bread is a mainstay of virtually every meal. Sometimes the bread is coated with *zatar*, a thyme-sumac-sesame seasoning which is easy to make or you can buy in specialist shops. I've also included a recipe for *fatayir* (*page 91*), smaller buns which in my version are stuffed with a tasty mixture of sesame, cheese and paprika; you can also try cooked spinach and sumac.

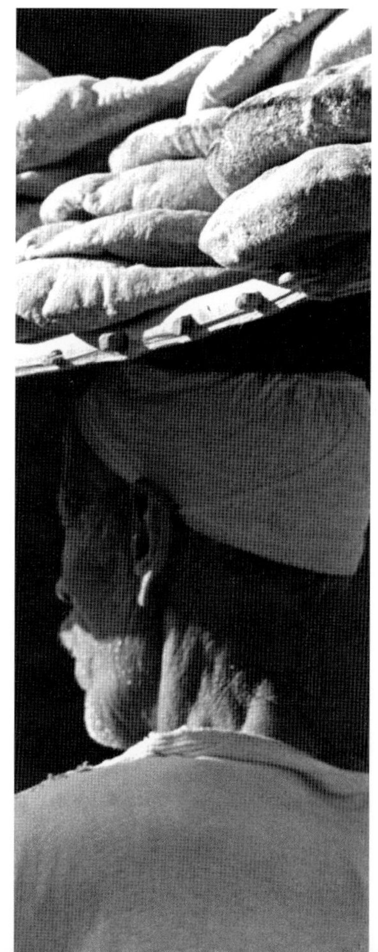

turkey

Vegetables are consumed in large quantities in the Turkish diet, giving rise to many vegetarian specialities. I adore *zeytinyagli*, a speciality of Turkish cuisine which, roughly translated, means 'olive oil course'. This is really a very simple dish where vegetables, such as courgettes or aubergines, are cooked very slowly in olive oil and gradually release their own juices. Once cooked, the vegetables have a melt-in-the-mouth texture. My recipe on page 98 is made with courgettes, but there are numerous variations made with green beans, artichokes and celery cooked in this way, often with mixtures of tomatoes, green peppers and onions. Served with chunks of crusty fresh bread, *zeytinyagli* is a perfect light summer meal.

Many recipes use well-known herbs such as mint and parsley. I've used them to flavour the tasty courgette and leek fritters on page 103. Another flavouring I was introduced to which has since become a firm favourite is *pul biber*, a hot red pepper with quite a bite. Sold dried and flaked, it is great sprinkled on vegetable purées and used with pulses.

greece

Olive trees flourish across Greece, and it is one of the world's largest producers of virgin olive oil. Hardly surprising that olives and their oil, along with aubergines, tomatoes, peppers and garlic, are fundamental elements of the Greek daily diet and are used to produce a wide variety of nourishing dishes. All these ingredients, combined in simple recipes, are enhanced by many native mountain-grown herbs such as oregano, mint, dill, basil, bay leaves, rosemary and thyme. Most of these herbs are generally used dried. They make a big difference to the classic Greek lentil soup on page 92, and dried mint perks up the rich cheese filling for *tyropitas* on page 109. Dill is a herb that is more often used fresh. It's great with artichokes in the simple casserole on page 112, and works just as well with tomato sauces. As a change you could also try flavouring tomato sauces with cinnamon, one of the sweeter spices widely used in Greece, along with nutmeg, to flavour both sweet and savoury dishes. The warm, dry climate also suits the lemon tree, which produces large fragrant fruit, and much typical Greek food is redolent with lemon flavours.

Yogurt is extensively used in Greek cuisine, mainly for dips and spreads. Tzatziki, the classic yogurt dish, is made from grated cucumber and garlic. Another common dairy product is feta, a brine-soaked cheese made from sheep's or sometimes goat's milk, which is aged in barrels or tins. It has a light but salty flavour which goes well with fresh ingredients such as tomatoes. The famous Greek salad consists of cubes of feta, tomatoes, cucumber and fresh black olives with dressing.

common ingredients and useful techniques

blossom water

Made with rose or orange blossom, this strongly perfumed water is sold in specialist shops. It is frequently used to flavour fruit dishes, puddings and sweets. Use sparingly a few drops at a time and then increase the amount according to taste.

bulgur wheat – fine and coarse

This is also known as cracked wheat. It is the wheat grain which has been cooked and dried, then crushed. Fine and coarse varieties are available. I find the coarse works best when it is to be cooked and served as a pilaff and the fine is what I use for soaking and serving in salads such as the classic *tabbouleh*.

coriander, mint, flat-leaf parsley

These three fresh herbs are used in abundance in this region for hot and cold dishes. They may be finely chopped in salads or mixed with grains, vegetables and bean purées. Try to find a specialist shop selling these herbs as they tend to be better value. Otherwise try growing your own.

pimenton

This spice is made from peppers which are oak-smoked, dried and ground. The resulting bright red powder has a distinctive flavour and smoky aroma.

pistachios

Pistachios have a brilliant green colour and slight almond flavour. Pick pistachio nuts which have a half-open shell; if closed, the nut isn't fully ripe and the shell is very hard to remove. Salted pistachios are for snacks, unsalted nuts are for both sweet and savoury recipes.

sumac

Sumac berries are tart, almost lemon-flavoured, dark red berries which are ground into a fine powder. The powder is sprinkled neat over rice and other grain dishes, mixed with chopped onion as a relish and with sesame seeds for a spice mixture called *zatar* (see below).

tahini or tahina

This is a paste made from sesame seeds rather like the sesame equivalent of peanut butter. Buy pale-coloured tahini and use it to thicken bean, lentil and vegetable purées or mix with yogurt and garlic for a simple dip.

zatar (zahtar)

A flavouring made from crushed sesame, thyme and sumac. Sprinkle it over cooked bread, vegetable and bean dishes, or mix with olive oil for a dip. Proportions vary, but use mostly sesame and add thyme and sumac to taste.

to stuff vine leaves

Open out the vine leaf and place a spoonful of filling at the point where the stalk meets the leaf. Fold the lower sides of the leaf over the filling so that they overlap. Then fold in the remaining sides of the leaf to make them in line with the edges of the filling – you should be looking at a rough rectangle. Roll the leaf from the base to the tip to create a neat package. When you are ready to cook, place them in a dish which will hold them in a single, tight-packed layer, with the folds underneath.

making yogurt

If you want to make all your yogurt, it's useful to have a commercial yogurt maker, but for an occasional batch, use a wide-necked thermos flask.

Heat 600ml (1 pint) milk to 43–45°C (110–115°F) Stir in a yogurt starter (either 2 tablespoons of natural live yogurt or a culture powder). Pour the mixture into a clean, warmed thermos flask. Leave overnight or until set then transfer to a clean container and refrigerate. For a thicker, richer yogurt, strain the mixture through a piece of muslin.

to blanch and skin almonds and pistachios

Place the nuts in a heatproof bowl, cover with boiling water, and leave to soak for a few minutes. Lift out of the hot water using a slotted spoon. As soon as you can handle the nuts, pinch the softened skin. The nuts should pop out of their skins when pressed. It is best to skin them whilst they remain warm; if they are allowed to cool again, the skin becomes harder to remove. Should any prove difficult to skin, put the nuts back in boiling water for a further few minutes.

'succulent and lemony, stuffed vine leaves are an attractive, versatile dish'

turkish breakfast

My mouth waters at the prospect of a full Turkish breakfast, a lovely mix of savouries, preserves and fruit – almost a cross between a European breakfast and brunch. Here are three recipes to help you create this meal. To complete the scene, have a good supply of chunks of fresh Turkish bread, which resemble crusty French loaves, bowls of jam, honey and yogurt, and a choice of fresh fruit – particularly water melon and fresh apricots in season.

turkish scrambled eggs

menemen

3 tbsp sunflower oil
1 onion, finely chopped
1 green pepper, deseeded and finely chopped
3 large tomatoes, finely chopped
4 eggs
4 tbsp finely chopped parsley
salt and pepper

1 In a medium pan heat the oil and fry the onion for 5–7 minutes or until fairly soft. Add the pepper and cook for a further 5 minutes stirring frequently, then add the tomatoes, mix in well then cover and cook for 5 minutes.

2 Remove the lid, stir and cook until the excess liquid has evaporated. Beat the eggs in a bowl and season. Add to the pan and cook for about 5 minutes stirring frequently to scramble the eggs.

3 Adjust the seasoning and stir in the chopped parsley. Serve hot.

cheese and walnut dip

muhammara

50g (2oz) walnuts
100g (3½oz) feta cheese
100g (3½oz) cream cheese
1–2 slices of stale white bread
2 cloves garlic
1–2 tbsp lemon juice
3 tbsp olive oil
¼ tsp dried chilli flakes
salt

1 Using a food processor, process the walnuts until ground to a coarse powder. Set aside in a small bowl.

2 Using the processor again, put in the feta cheese, cream cheese, bread and garlic. Blend until smooth, then add the ground walnuts, lemon juice, olive oil and dried chilli to taste. Season with salt if necessary.

3 The final consistency should be like thick yogurt. Leave to stand for the flavours to develop.

carrot dip

havuç ezmesi

3 carrots, peeled
2 tbsp olive oil
1 clove garlic, finely chopped
200g (7oz) Greek yogurt
salt and pepper

1 Coarsely grate the carrots. Heat the oil and gently fry the carrots with the garlic until they are very soft and slightly browned, stirring frequently.

2 Remove the pan from the heat and leave to cool and then stir in the yogurt and season to taste.

'It's easy to provide this lazy brunch for family and friends. Just imagine the clear blue sky and dazzling sea.

lebanese yeasted pastry with toppings

fatayir

When, in more northerly parts of Europe, commuters are rushing to work with their croissant and coffee, the early risers in the Lebanon are grabbing a couple of these yeasted pastries to have with their tea (either mint or black). There are numerous toppings and fillings to make. I have suggested a piquant chilli flavoured filling, but you can use spinach flavoured with sumac, olive oil and lemon juice, or zatar which is thyme, sumac and sesame mixed.

MAKES 10–12

FOR THE YEASTED PASTRY

450g (1lb) plain flour
1 sachet dried yeast
pinch of salt
1–2 tbsp sunflower oil
150ml (5fl oz) warm water

FOR THE FILLING

1 onion, finely grated
1 tbsp plain flour
1 tbsp paprika
1/2 tsp chilli powder (mild)
1 tbsp cream cheese
1 tbsp sesame seeds
1 tbsp tomato puree
3 tbsp olive oil
3 tbsp sunflower oil
salt

1 In a large bowl, mix the flour, yeast and a pinch of salt. Mix in the oil thoroughly with your fingers so that it is worked through the flour. Add enough water to make a soft dough which should be flexible but not sticky. Knead well then break into walnut-size balls and place on an oiled baking tray. Cover and leave to rise while you make the filling.

2 For the filling, mix all the ingredients together.

Press the risen dough into flat rounds with a 1-cm (1/2-inch) dent in the centre. Put spoonfuls of the filling in the hollow.

3 Heat the oven to 200°C (400°F) Gas Mark 6, then turn down to 180°C (350°F) Gas Mark 4 and put the pastries in to bake. Bake for 15 minutes or until crisp.

greek lentil soup

fakes

Soups in both Greece and Turkey are cooked in a different way from the French or English tradition in that the vegetables are boiled in the pan rather than being first sweated in oil or butter. The natural sweetness of the vegetables is more evident and a final burst of flavour is added at the end when a mixture of oil and vinegar is added. Use a well-flavoured olive oil for the best results.

SERVES 4–6

1 onion, finely chopped
2 sticks celery, finely diced
3 large carrots, finely diced
1 leek, cleaned and chopped
50g (2oz) whole brown lentils
900ml ($1\frac{1}{2}$ pint) water
1 bay leaf
1 sprig of rosemary
1 clove garlic, roughly crushed
3–4 tbsp olive oil
1–2 tsp white vinegar
salt

1 Prepare all the vegetables and place in a pan with the lentils, water, bay leaf, rosemary and garlic.

2 Bring to the boil and simmer for 1 hour or longer until the vegetables and lentils are very soft and starting to break up in the liquid. Mash the vegetables in the pan a little for a thicker consistency.

3 Stir in the olive oil, vinegar to taste and add salt to taste.

4 Serve warm with crusty bread.

mezze

Mezze consist of small dishes offered as appetizers before the main meal. Mezze are often served at large social gatherings where people have plenty of time to eat, drink and chat and the food on offer certainly helps the general ambience.

In the Lebanon, the simplest mezze might just include flat Arabic bread (pitta), hummus (the classic chickpea dip), baba ghanoush (a smooth silky dip made from chargrilled or smoked aubergine and tahini) and tabbouleh, which is featured on page 111. For really elaborate occasions, though, a Lebanese mezze might consist of a huge array of 40 or 50 different little dishes.

In Turkey, if there is a long formal meal, the mezze are sometimes divided into two courses, with cold dishes served first followed by hot dishes. Food comes on large platters to be shared by everyone, adding to the social atmosphere of the meal. These are eaten until the main course is served, along with wine or more likely with *raki* – the aniseed-flavoured national drink, sometimes referred to as 'lion's milk'. On less grand occasions the basic mezze might be slices of honeydew melon with feta cheese and freshly baked bread. There might also be *zeytinyagli*, savoury pastries, salads of cucumber and tomato and bowls of yogurt.

In Greece, the little dishes called *mezethes* are also served in order to help the drink along. This has been the tradition since the Ancient Greeks who found that drinking on an empty stomach was not a sensible idea. It became customary to serve *mezethes* wherever and whenever alcohol was offered. A varied mezze selection might include contrasting individual dishes such as stuffed vine leaves, small bite-size pastries, simple cubes of cheese or crisp radishes.

I use the mezze idea for a substantial first course as well as brunch fare, picnics and buffet feasts. This chapter features over a dozen different ideas and there are also recipes in the North Africa section that can be used, such as the red pepper dip on page 128 and the salads on pages 140, 142 and 143.

Mix and match all these recipes to create contrasting flavours, textures and colours. It is less daunting in preparation than it sounds, as much of the food – certainly dips, dishes with pulses, rissoles or stuffed vine leaves – benefit from being made in advance. It is good to have a plentiful supply of crusty bread or pitta bread to serve with the food.

Apart from the recipes given in this chapter, here are some other ideas you might come across or be able to make, so that you can ring the changes on what is sure to be a very successful meal:

tzatziki, a delicious yogurt and cucumber salad made with thick yogurt, grated cucumber, crushed garlic and chopped fresh or dried mint. This is often served with slices of fried aubergine or courgette and olives.

skordalia, a pungent thick sauce which is more appetizing than it sounds! It is made from soaked breadcrumbs mixed with oil, ground walnuts and plenty of garlic, which gives it bite. The final consistency is similar to mayonnaise.

greek salad, a classic mixture of cubed feta, with fresh tomatoes, green pepper, cucumber and black olives, flavoured with oregano and dressed with olive oil.

falafel, small deep-fried patties made of highly spiced ground chickpeas.

hummus, the classic dip made from a purée of cooked chickpeas mixed with olive oil, tahini, lemon and garlic.

borek, filo pastry filled with spinach and cheese.

çoban salatsi (shepherd's salad), a diced salad of tomato, green pepper, spring onion, cucumber, basil and coriander with an olive oil and lemon dressing.

fried aubergine slices, served with yogurt and garlic sauce.

fried aubergine, with red chilli pepper served with chopped onion and roasted red pepper dip.

piyaz, a haricot bean salad with hard-boiled eggs, grated carrot, shredded red cabbage and onion.

cacik, grated cucumber with yogurt, garlic and salt, sprinkled with dill and olive oil.

stuffed vine leaves

warak enab b'zeit

I was surprised to learn that my Lebanese friends used a raw rice for stuffing vine leaves as I had always made versions where the rice is cooked first. The advantage of this method is that not only is a stage saved in the cooking process but the grains swell during the cooking and create a really well-filled parcel. Do chop the onion, herbs and tomatoes very finely so they mix easily with the rice.

MAKES ABOUT 25

125g (4oz) raw rice (short grain or risotto variety)
1 small onion, very finely chopped
4 tbsp finely chopped fresh parsley
4 tbsp finely chopped fresh coriander
2 tomatoes, very finely chopped
50g (2oz) pine nuts
2–3 tbsp olive oil
1–2 tbsp lemon juice
1 tsp lemon zest
vine leaves

1 In a large bowl, mix all the ingredients, apart from the vine leaves, and season well.

2 Put a spoonful into each vine leaf at the stalk end, then fold over the sides and roll up from the stalk end very tightly.

3 Using a large wide saucepan, arrange the stuffed vine leaves in circles starting at the centre and working outwards. Cover with boiling water.

4 Weigh down with a plate.

5 Cook very slowly for about 45–60 minutes until done.

6 The only way to ascertain this is to break one open after about 45 minutes, then check about every 10 minutes or so.

7 Leave to cool.

courgettes and carrots in olive oil

zeytinyagli kabak

In summer, *zeytinyagli* dishes are made in almost every Turkish home. These are mixtures of vegetables slowly cooked in olive oil, sometimes left to stand overnight, then eaten cold with fresh crusty bread as a separate course or a light lunch. Courgettes, carrots, artichokes, green and white beans work well.

SERVES 4

3 or 4 medium courgettes
1 carrot
1 medium onion
2–3 cloves garlic, chopped
4 tomatoes, roughly chopped
2 tbsp tomato purée
1 tsp sugar
4 tbsp olive oil
salt and pepper

1 Trim the courgettes and cut into thick finger-size pieces.

2 Peel the carrot and cut into thick sticks,

3 Halve the onion and slice each half thickly.

4 Heat the oil in a pan and then add the onion slices with the garlic and sticks of carrot.

5 Cook the vegetables slowly over a gentle heat, stirring occasionally. As they begin to soften add the courgettes and tomatoes and cook for a few minutes more. Mix the tomato purée with 100ml (3½fl oz) water, add to the pan and stir in with the sugar. Season well. Bring to the boil and simmer very slowly until the sauce has reduced and the vegetables are soft. Season to taste. Leave to cool.

red lentil and bulgur rissoles

mercimek koftesi

These mini rissoles are best made in advance for the flavours to develop. Ensure the red lentils cook to a soft purée and are not too sloppy. Don't panic at the amount of parsley; it gives both colour and flavour. Delicious served with yogurt, either plain or mixed with crushed garlic and salt, if you wish.

MAKES 24

150g (5oz) red lentils, rinsed
125g (4oz) bulgur wheat
125ml (4fl oz) olive oil
1 large onion, finely diced
1/4 –1/2 tsp dried chilli flakes
2 tsp ground cumin
1 tbsp tomato purée
6 spring onions, finely chopped
125g (4oz) finely chopped fresh parsley
salt

1 Using a large saucepan, bring the lentils to the boil with 300ml (1/2 pint) water, then cover the pan and simmer for 15–20 minutes. Beat the mixture in the pan with a wooden spoon and if the purée is very sloppy, cook for a little longer but do not let it become dry. It will firm a little on cooling.

2 Add the bulgur wheat which will absorb excess water. Cover, leave to cool.

3 Heat the oil and fry the onion with the chilli flakes until translucent and soft. Stir in the ground cumin and cook for 2–3 minutes longer.

4 Mix the cooked onions into the lentil and bulgur wheat mix and add the tomato purée, spring onions and chopped parsley. Season to taste.

5 Shape the mixture with your hands into small ovals roughly the size that will fit in the palm.

6 Arrange on a serving plate and serve at room temperature with yogurt.

brown lentil and rice dip

moujadara

As my Lebanese friend noted 'this dish is nothing until the final flavourings are put in'. You cook the lentils then the rice is stirred in to cook gradually – resulting in a soft thick mixture. This simple dish is lifted by the fried onion flavour and the acidity of the pickles acts as a perfect foil to the earthy pulses. It benefits from being left to stand for several hours before serving.

SERVES 4–6

250g (8oz) brown lentils, rinsed
100g (3½oz) round grain rice (risotto rice)
1 large onion, finely chopped
2–3 tbsp olive oil
salt and pepper

FOR THE GARNISH OR SIDE SALAD
½ cucumber, chopped
2 spring onions, chopped
2 tomatoes, chopped

1 Cook the lentils in a medium pan in double their volume of water until quite soft.

2 Add the rice and stir frequently until the rice is soft adding more water gradually during the cooking process, keeping the heat low so that the mixture does not burn. You may need to add up to 250–300ml (8–10fl oz) as the final consistency needs to be soft.

3 In a separate pan, heat the oil and fry the onion slowly until brown, stir into the lentil and rice mixture and leave to cool.

4 Season well.

5 Serve with a side salad of chopped cucumber, spring onion and tomato, pitta bread and pickles such as pickled turnip.

TIMESAVER *Home-made pickled turnip would be within the culinary repertoire of many Lebanese cooks, but you can buy it in specialist food shops and delicatessens if you want to keep the accompaniments authentic.*

courgette and leek fritters

mücver

Mücver are mouth-watering little fritters eaten as a snack between lunch and supper. They can be part of a mezze spread as they are good warm or hot, or serve a pile of them with bread and salads to make a meal.

MAKES 48
LITTLE FRITTERS

2 eggs
125ml (4fl oz) yogurt
100g (3½oz) crumbled feta
1 tsp baking powder
2 tbsp finely chopped fresh parsley
1 tbsp finely chopped fresh mint
salt and pepper
3 tbsp plain flour
250g (8oz) courgettes, finely diced
250g (8oz) leeks, very finely chopped

1 In a large bowl, beat the eggs and stir in the yogurt, crumbled feta, baking powder and herbs. Add the flour and mix well. Season to taste.

2 Add the courgettes and leeks to the egg and herb mixture.

3 Lightly oil a large baking sheet and drop on heaped teaspoons of the mixture, flattening slightly.

4 Bake at 200°C (400°F) Gas Mark 6 for 15 minutes then flip over and cook for a further 2–3 minutes until lightly browned.

toasted pitta bread salad

fattouch

This is a fresh, colourful, flavoursome salad. The main ingredients are parsley, mint, spring onion and tomatoes but other ingredients such as radishes, and variously coloured peppers can be added. Texture comes from crisply toasted pitta bread croûtons which are then drizzled with olive oil and sprinkled with the lemony flavoured sumac which add more colour and flavour. If you can't get sumac from a Middle East speciality shop or good supermarket, either leave the bread plain or grind over a little black pepper.

SERVES 4–6

8 spring onions
1 cucumber
3–4 tomatoes
150g (5oz) finely chopped fresh parsley
75g (3oz) finely chopped fresh mint
12 radishes
1 yellow pepper (could be red or green)
2 pitta breads
5 tbsp olive oil
1 tsp sumac
1 cos lettuce
4–6 tbsp lemon juice

1 Finely chop the spring onions, and cut the cucumber and tomatoes into small dice. Put into a large bowl and mix in the herbs.

2 Slice the radishes, dice the pepper and mix both in with the other salad ingredients.

3 Slice the pitta breads in half and toast under the grill until crisp and brown on both sides.

4 Drizzle over a little olive oil and sprinkle the bread with sumac.

5 Just before serving mix the salad ingredients with lemon juice, olive oil and bread.

6 Serve the salad with cos lettuce leaves. The aim is to serve the salad while the bread is still crisp.

aubergine dip

salatet batenjan

Aubergine dips and purées are popular in Middle Eastern cuisine, perhaps the best known being *baba ghanoush* which is cooked aubergine enriched with tahini. This one uses grilled aubergines mixed with clean-tasting green peppers, tomatoes and a clove or two of garlic. It is simple to make and keeps well if you need to make it in advance. If the tomatoes are very juicy or watery hold back on some of the liquid or you may make the dip too sloppy.

SERVES 4–6

1 large or two medium aubergines
2 tomatoes
1 green pepper, chopped very finely
1–2 tbsp lemon juice
4–6 tbsp olive oil
1–2 cloves garlic, crushed
salt and pepper
chopped parsley, to garnish

1 Slice the aubergines in half lengthways, Grill the aubergine for about 5 minutes, then turn over and grill the other side. Turn again and repeat this process checking to see if the aubergine is quite soft. Grill for longer if necessary. Leave to cool, then remove the peel.

2 Mash in a pestle and mortar or process in a food processor until fairly smooth. Quarter the tomatoes and remove the seeds, then chop finely. Add them with the remaining ingredients to the aubergine. Mash or process until the purée has a fairly smooth texture.

3 Season well and serve garnished with parsley

white bean salad

fasoulia b'zeit

This recipe is one of a family of dishes made in a similar way to the Turkish *zeytinyagli* (*see page 98*). *Loubyen b'zeit* is made with green beans in a tomato and garlic mixture; *bamieh b'zeit* is okra cooked with lashings of olive oil and tomatoes and flavoured with coriander. This version uses white beans such as haricot, butter beans, or lima beans which are like a baby butter bean.

SERVES 4

200g (7oz) white beans – haricot, lima beans, or small butter beans
6 tbsp olive oil
1 onion, finely chopped or 3 spring onions, finely chopped
2 cloves garlic, chopped
2 tbsp lemon juice
4 tbsp finely chopped parsley
salt and pepper

1 Soak the beans overnight in a large bowl of cold water. Drain and rinse well then bring to the boil in a large pan of fresh water.

2 Boil fiercely for 10 minutes and then reduce the heat, cover the pan and simmer for 30–40 minutes or until the beans are tender.

3 Drain off any excess water (which can be saved and used for stock) and set aside.

4 Heat the oil and cook the onion and garlic for a few minutes, then add the warm beans and cook slowly for 10 minutes stirring gently so that the beans absorb the flavour.

5 Remove from the heat and add the lemon juice and seasoning to taste. Then stir in the fresh parsley and leave to cool.

feta cheese and mint pastries

tyropitas

Many pastry dishes in Greece are now made with filo pastry but in the villages far from shops, flaky pastry is still used for these little savouries. The crust is a bit thicker and because of that they are not shaped in triangular fashion but either in half moons or boat shapes. If you want to save time use ready-made filo pastry.

MAKES 12–16

FOR THE PASTRY

250g (8oz) plain flour
150g (5oz) vegetable fat or butter
1 tbsp lemon juice
120ml (4fl oz) ice cold water

FOR THE BÉCHAMEL SAUCE

25g (1oz) butter
25g (1oz) plain flour
150ml (5fl oz) milk

250g (8oz) feta cheese, mashed
1–2 tbsp dried mint
salt and black pepper
beaten egg yolk, to glaze

1 To make the pastry, put the flour in a large bowl and grate in the cold fat, then add the lemon juice and water gradually and draw into a rough ball. Wrap the dough in clingfilm and chill for 30 minutes.

2 To make the sauce, melt the butter and stir in the flour to make a roux, cook for 1–2 minutes then pour over the milk and bring gradually to the boil, stirring all the time. When the sauce is thick, cook for 2 minutes and then season a little, remember that the feta is salty, and leave to cool.

3 Use enough of the sauce to mash into the feta to make a moist mixture then stir in the mint and season if necessary.

4 Roll out the pastry thinly and cut into 20-cm (8-inch) rounds (or smaller, if you wish to make more). Put a heaped spoonful of mixture in the centre and bring up either side and pinch together in a pasty shape. Alternatively, make half moons and seal the edges well with cold water. Brush with a little beaten egg to glaze.

5 Bake at 200°C (400°F) Gas Mark 6 for 15–20 minutes. Serve warm or cold.

chickpea and aubergine casserole

moussakaat batenjan

Although known as moussaka this bears little resemblance to the Greek recipe of that name except that it contains aubergine. In this Lebanese dish, the aubergine is cooked with an onion and garlic mixture then combined with chickpeas and tomato sauce. It is easy and very tasty. Once again, designed to be eaten cold and often best prepared several hours ahead so that the flavours have time to develop.

SERVES 4

3–4 tbsp olive oil
1 onion, chopped
1 head garlic, peeled and chopped
2 large aubergines
1 x 400g (14oz) can chickpeas, drained and rinsed
1 x 400g (14oz) can chopped tomatoes
salt and pepper

1 In a large pan, heat the oil and gently fry the onion and garlic until browned.

2 Trim the stalk end of the aubergines and then either peel entirely or simply peel strips creating a striped effect, then cut the aubergines into thick slices.

3 Put the aubergine on top of the onion and garlic mixture and fry for a few minutes, then cover with the chickpeas, and pour over the tomatoes.

4 Bring the mixture to the boil and then cover the pan and simmer for 10 minutes. Season well. Leave to cool.

bulgur wheat salad

tabbouleh

This is a classic salad that can be made in numerous different ways. In the Lebanon, parsley and mint are the main ingredients with fine bulgur wheat used to soak up juice from the tomatoes and the dressing, thus strengthening the overall flavour of the dish. You can make your version densely green such as this, or add a little more bulgur wheat if you prefer. In the Lebanon, tabbouleh is often eaten spooned into fresh young vine leaves, or cos lettuce, or white cabbage leaves.

SERVES 4–6

450g (1lb) tomatoes, cut into smal dice
50g (2oz) bulgur wheat
175–250g (6–8oz) fresh parsley
125g (4oz) fresh mint
1 bunch spring onions
1 clove garlic, finely chopped
juice of 1–2 lemons
100ml (3½fl oz) olive oil
salt and pepper

1 Put all the tomato pulp and juice into a large bowl and stir in the bulgur wheat. Leave to soak for 30 minutes or longer.

2 Finely chop the herbs and spring onions.

3 Stir the herbs and garlic into the bulgur wheat and tomato mixture and add the lemon juice and olive oil.

4 Season to taste.

fresh peas with artichokes

arakas me aginares

This is a simple vegetable dish that can be served as either a side vegetable or served mezze-style along with a choice of other dishes.

SERVES 4

4 artichoke hearts
juice of 1 lemon
3 tbsp olive oil
1 onion, finely chopped
2 cloves garlic, finely chopped
450g (1lb) passata
2 tsp chopped fresh dill
250g (8oz) fresh or frozen peas
salt and pepper

1 To prepare the artichoke hearts, cut away all of the coarse outer leaves and leave behind only the tender parts of the inner leaves. Have ready a bowl of acidulated water (cold water with juice of a lemon added). Cut the artichokes in half and carefully remove the inedible choke, immediately the artichokes are prepared drop them in the water to prevent them discolouring. Leave soaking while the other ingredients are prepared.

2 In a large saucepan, heat the oil and cook the onions and garlic over a low heat until soft. Add the artichokes and cook for 10 minutes. Add the passata and dill bring to the boil and simmer for 5 minutes. Add the peas and cook for 3–4 minutes or until the peas are just tender.

3 Season well and serve hot or cold.

pistachio and sultana cake with orange syrup

halweyat

Bright green pistachio nuts are frequently used in sweet dishes from this region. They have a pleasing flavour and a good crunchy texture which contrasts well with the sweet, sticky fruitiness of this moreish cake.

MAKES 12–16

175g (6oz) butter, melted
2 eggs
175g (6oz) golden or white caster sugar
200g (7oz) thick yogurt
½tsp vanilla extract
250g (8oz) self-raising flour
½tsp baking powder
75g (3oz) sultanas
75g (3oz) pistachio nuts
1 tsp orange zest

FOR THE SYRUP

140g (5oz) white caster sugar
4 tbsp water
3 tbsp orange juice
2 tbsp lemon juice

1 Line a deep-sided baking tray 18x28cm (7x11 inches) with baking parchment.

2 Melt the butter and leave to cool.

3 In a large bowl, cream the eggs and sugar until pale and thick. This takes about 4 minutes.

4 In a separate bowl, beat the cooled melted butter with the yogurt and vanilla extract, and stir into the egg and sugar mixture.

5 Sift in the flour and baking powder and gently fold in with the sultanas, pistachio nuts and orange zest.

6 Pour into the lined tray and bake for 35–40 minutes at 180°C (350°F) Gas Mark 4 or until golden brown and springy to the touch.

7 For the orange syrup, dissolve the sugar in the water and then simmer for 5 minutes. Add 3 tablespoons of orange juice and 1–2 tablespoons of lemon juice.

8 When the cake is cooked and cooling, bring the syrup back to the boil and then pour slowly and evenly over the cake.

fig and apricot compôte

komposto

Turkey has an abundance of fresh fruits such as figs and apricots and many are preserved by drying to last through the winter. Once stewed with flavourings, these *komposto* make gorgeous yet simple desserts, delicious on their own or served with dollops of thick yogurt.

SERVES 4–6

125g (4oz) dried figs
125g (4oz) dried apricots
75g (3oz) sultanas
½tbsp cornflour
¼tsp turmeric
50g (2oz) hazelnuts, chopped (roasted)

1 Cut the figs and apricots into bite size pieces and put into a medium pan with the sultanas.

2 Mix the cornflour with a little cold water then add another 350ml (12fl oz) water. Stir in the turmeric and pour the liquid over the dried fruit.

3 Bring the mixture to the boil and then cover the pan and cook over a gentle heat for about 30–40 minutes then leave to cool.

4 Once cold, spoon into individual glasses or an attractive bowl and decorate with coarsely chopped hazelnuts.

africa

When my Moroccan friend first arrived to cook with me, it was as if the travelling *souk* or market had landed in the porch as she stood on the doorstep with a sack of flour, bags of spices and a selection of enormous cooking dishes. Within minutes, it seems, my house was filled with a rich spicy aroma and in the warmth of the kitchen there were glistening dough balls covered with olive oil, waiting to be miraculously stretched into featherlight layered pastries, which we later munched dripping with honey. Wheel-shaped discs of dough covered an entire work surface, rising under thick towels, ready to be cooked in a huge round heavy-bottomed pan. I ground quantities of black pepper, salted lemons, and raked through bowls of couscous with my fingertips separating the creamy grains. Commonplace ingredients such as carrots, potatoes, beetroots and leeks, split peas and beans were transformed into colourful, flavourful dips, salads, dressings and main courses.

The northern part of Africa, along the Mediterranean from Morocco to Egypt, is part of the Mediterranean culinary rim, as well as acting as a geographical link that connects Africa and the Arab world with Europe and the West. Hundreds of years ago, North Africa became a crossroads for the spice trade. From east to west and north to south, the spice caravans would arrive with caraway and saffron from Arabia, ginger from China and black pepper and sugar from India. Spices from the New World included cayenne and allspice. From the north came Romans with mustard, who also planted the region with olive groves.

It is hardly surprising, given the history of the region, that spices are used at virtually every meal and seemingly in every type of food. Cooking oils, dips and breads are all laden with spices. There are scented desserts, aromatic pastries and spiced drinks. Coffee is blended with green cardamom pods, and dried mint leaves are steeped for tea.

the spice crossroads

Vegetables and various grains, such as wheat, rice, corn, millet and barley, form the staple diet here. The grains are either made into couscous or a variety of leavened and unleavened flat breads. As in the rest of the Arab world, bread is an indispensable part of the meal and is used for scooping food and mopping up sauces or for dipping into purées, harissa or olive oil. Vegetables are eaten in all manner of ways – raw, pickled, grilled, puréed into dips, stuffed, or added to stews, soups or grains as starters, main meals and accompaniments. Amongst my favourite dishes are the salads made from raw vegetables; if cooked, the cooled vegetables are served at room temperature. The flavours are as easy to savour as the glowing colours are to appreciate – for an example, see the carrot and beetroot salad on page 140.

Another trait I find highly appealing in this part of the world is the use of sweet ingredients such as fresh and dried fruit to complement savoury foods and temper hot spices. Apricots and raisins are often added to vegetables and sauces for couscous or tagines, or are cooked with a single vegetable, as, for example, in the spiced cabbage and raisin dish on page 141. I discovered that dates are served with the traditional bean and vegetable soup of these countries, *harrira* (*see page 127*). In addition to being completely delicious, you'll find the sweetness of the fruit counteracts the fiery taste of the black pepper.

North African meals range across the entire culinary spectrum – from the very simple and mildly flavoured or scented to complex dishes that are richly spiced and fiery to taste. Slowly simmered stews, or tagines, where the flavours have plenty of time to develop are commonplace. The basic flavourings are usually garlic along with many other different types of onion, including red onion, spring onion and leeks.

The key to all dishes that identify North African cooking is the use of spices. Many of the recipes featured in this section make use of quite simple but very effective taste combinations based on cumin, paprika and black pepper. These three spices can be added in varying proportions to create a surprising range of flavours. To obtain a more complex taste, I have added chillies, ginger and turmeric to some of the recipes. In the couscous recipe on page 138, for example, the spices used include the standard trio plus coriander seed and cinnamon, as well as fresh herbs such as coriander and parsley. The taste is sublime.

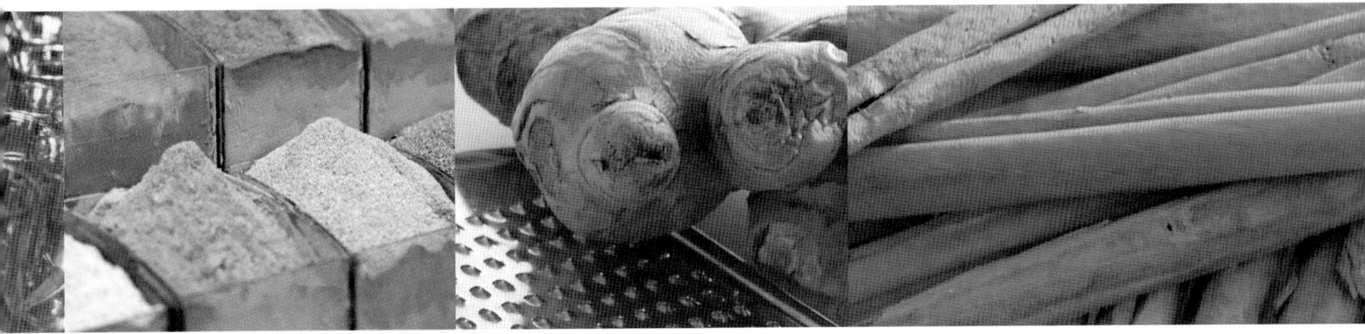

The more elaborate the spice mixture, the harder it is to ensure the flavours are properly balanced. Morocco, Tunisia, Ethiopia and Egypt all have at least one or two signature blends which dramatically alter the character of a dish. Spice mixtures in these countries are sold ready-made or even made to order. If you travel to this part of the world, it is well worth buying spice mixtures where the balancing act has been done for you. I have found spice mixes in specialist shops from a variety of suppliers and the flavours vary quite considerably. Experiment to see what you like or, if you want to make your own, start by using more of your favourite spice. Here are some of the most popular mixes.

Ras el hanout: This is the name given in Morocco to the classic spice blend which means 'top of the shop' (supposedly because the shop owners would make up unique blends, using their choice of spice). It can include some 20 or more ingredients and will be specially prepared according to the shopkeeper and the type of dish that is to be flavoured. The daunting array of spices may include cinnamon, black peppercorns, green cardamom, caraway, nutmeg and rosebuds.

Harissa: This condiment is widely used in Morocco, Algeria and Tunisia. It is basically a deep red paste made from chillies that can be exceptionally fiery or tempered with milder aromatics. It is possible to make your own simple version, see page 125, but it is also sold in small jars, pots or tubes in specialist shops and larger supermarkets.

Berbere: A basic Ethiopian mix of highly aromatic and hot spices including garlic, red chillies, fresh ginger, basil, red onions and cinnamon.

Baharat: This is quite similar to the spices used in the potato and olive tagine (*page 133*). It is quite aromatic and usually contains cinnamon, cumin, allspice and paprika.

Tunisian five-spice: If you prefer an aromatic rather than a hot flavour it is worth trying some of the tagines that incorporate the classic Tunisian five-spice mixture, which usually contains pepper as well as cinnamon, nutmeg and cloves.

common ingredients and useful techniques

The three fundamental spices of North Africa: cumin, paprika and black peppercorns

aniseed

This spice has a warm liquorice taste and is a good flavouring in bread.

black pepper

Pepper is one of the world's oldest and most popular spices. Peppercorns were once more valuable than gold and were used in the Middle Ages as currency. The hot, spicy 'corns' give an intense flavour. Freshly ground black pepper is used in quite large quantities, but is added at the start of cooking so the spice has time to cook thoroughly.

cayenne

A member of the red chilli family, so named because of its origins in the Cayenne region of French Guyana. After drying, the pods and seeds are ground together to give a hot and spicy taste.

cinnamon

This spice comes from the inner bark of a small tree. The quills or sticks can be used whole when stewing a savoury mixture or fruit compôte. Cinnamon adds a delicate fragrance, and a slightly sweet, warm taste.

cumin

Cumin seeds are brownish yellow and boat-shaped. This pungent, warming spice has a wonderful aroma when freshly ground. Used whole, the seeds need lightly roasting to bring out the flavour.

ginger

Ginger gives a sweet, fiery taste to food and is often paired with black pepper, especially in tagines.

paprika

Another member of the red chilli family. It is a brick-red powder with a warm rather than hot taste.

turmeric

Turmeric comes from the root of a tropical plant that is related to ginger. It has a warm, mild taste but also acts as a natural food colour, adding a pleasant golden glow.

tagine

Long-simmering stews or sauces are called tagines in North Africa, and are cooked in a covered dish confusingly also called a tagine. The traditional tagine is an earthenware pot, topped with a conical lid.

couscous

Couscous is made from tiny balls of semolina flour and this grain has given its name to the Moroccan national dish, but it is also popular in Tunisia and Algeria.

Traditional cooks prepare couscous by moistening the grains and steaming them over a special cooking pot called a *couscousière* – a two-piece pot. The lower part holds the stew and the upper part has a tight-fitting sieve that holds the couscous grains: the vegetable broth cooks slowly and aromatic steam rises through the sieve to cook the couscous. The cooked grains plump up to three times their original size. Before serving, *smen* [preserved butter] or butter is added to separate the grains and give them a soft, fluffy texture and rich flavour.

Unless you have a *couscousière,* you can use a large pan and a good-fitting sieve. Instructions on packets of couscous might well suggest microwaving or boiling the couscous, but it is far better to steam it and better still to steam it not once, but twice. This may sound a chore, but it is quick and easy and can be done well ahead of time.

Wash the couscous until clear in several changes of water to remove the starch, then pour the couscous into a steamer, forming a slight mound. The base of the steamer or sieve should not be in contact with the water. Steam for about 6–8 minutes, uncovered. Check that the grain has swelled.

Remove from the heat, tip onto a plate and sprinkle with cold water and some salt. Then add 1 tablespoon oil and work through the couscous with your hands to break up any lumps, and separate the grains with a fork or your fingertips. Steam the grains again just before serving.

Couscous presentation varies among regions. It can be served very moist with vegetables spooned over the grain, or in a mound with the vegetables put in the middle and then mixed together at the table.

accompaniments

North Africa boasts numerous preserves, condiments, sauces and other accompaniments that enhance and complement classic dishes. Three of the most popular are featured here. Olives you can buy; the others you can either make at home or look for in specialist food shops.

olives

Morocco is one of the world's largest producers of olives. They were brought by Greek colonizers from Sicily and, as trade routes developed, the Romans planted vast olive groves across North Africa. The olives grown around Fes and Meknes are thought to be some of the best.

All fresh olives are bitter and tough and must be cured before they are edible. Once harvested, they are sorted according to colour and size and then cured. In Morocco, there are dozens of ways to cure olives and they are sold and used at many different stages of ripeness. Colours range from unripe and green through red and purple and finally ripe and black. Olives can be prepared with different types of vinegar, spices or mixed with different vegetables, including small onions or carrots. In the markets of Morocco, an impressive array of olives is sold directly from enormous barrels.

Salted black olives are very different from marinated or brine-soaked olives as they have undergone an entirely different curing process. These olives have a wrinkled, leathery appearance with a concentrated flavour from the dry-salt curing process.

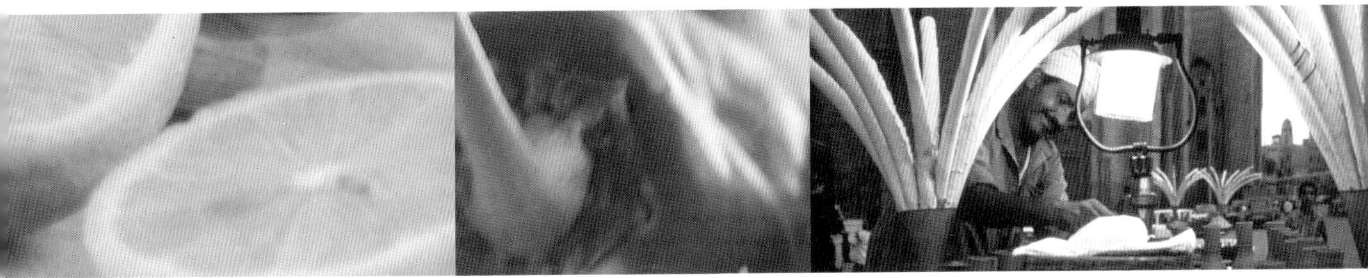

preserved lemons

The preserved lemon is quite different from the mouth-puckeringly sharp fresh lemon. Lemons are preserved in the spring when they are at their sweetest and ripest. The preserving process mellows the fruit and gives it an almost silken texture. In Morocco, preserved lemons are sold loose in the markets or *souks*. It is possible to buy them from specialist shops, but it is also quite simple to try making your own.

Have ready a small to medium clean jar. Quarter the lemons (12–15 will probably fit in the jar) by cutting through almost to the stem end and pack the cut surfaces with plenty of salt – leave overnight in a bowl to drain. This starts the shrinking process and makes them easier to pack in the jar. The following day, pack the lemons into the prepared jar and pour over any juice. Fill the jar to the brim with fresh lemon juice and then seal the jar. Store for about three weeks before using. Preserved in this way, the lemons will keep for a very long time. Preserved lemons can be left completely plain, but in some regions it is traditional to add cinnamon sticks, cloves and coriander for an alternative taste. When adding preserved lemons to dishes, typically the peel and juice are used. Preserved lemons can also be mixed with olives and cubes of cheese and served as part of a mezze.

harissa

This is a fiery paste (rather like the Indonesian 'sambal olek') which basically consists of hot chillies, garlic, olive oil and salt. Many variations are possible which include spices such as cumin, coriander, or other flavourings such as lime juice.

To make your own paste you can soak some dried chillies until soft and then drain and pound in a pestle and mortar. Add some garlic and salt and pound again to a purée, then mix with olive oil and store in a clean jar in the refrigerator. Harissa is served as a dipping sauce and with salads. It can be diluted with olive oil and lemon juice.

bean and vegetable soup

harrira

This is a delicious, nourishing soup traditionally eaten with dates to break the fast of Ramadan. It has a variety of beans and a few fresh vegetables though each family may add what they have on hand. Towards the end of the cooking process, the soup is thickened with flour to give it a smooth, thick character. It is best to use dried pulses and remember to soak them overnight, They can all be cooked together and this process means you also have plenty of stock.

SERVES 4–6

125g (4oz) chickpeas
50g (2oz) green lentils
4 tbsp olive oil
2 large onions, chopped
4 sticks celery, chopped
1 cinnamon stick
1 tsp turmeric
1–2 tbsp ground black pepper
400g (14oz) can chopped tomatoes
1 tbsp tomato purée
1 tbsp plain flour
25–40g (1–1½oz) vermicelli
3–4 tbsp chopped fresh coriander
3–4 tbsp chopped fresh parsley
salt

TO SERVE

lemon wedges, dates, bread

1 Soak pulses together overnight and then drain and rinse well. Place in a large saucepan filled with cold water. Bring to the boil, boil fast for 10 minutes and then reduce the heat and cook for 45 minutes or until fairly soft. Drain and reserve the stock.

2 Heat the oil and cook the onions with the celery and spices. Add the cooked pulses, tomatoes, tomato purée and 1 litre (1¾ pints) stock. Cook for 20 minutes then add more stock if necessary. Add the flour by making it into a paste first with some of the soup and stirring it into the soup gradually to create a thick velvet texture,

3 Add the vermicelli and cook for about 5 minutes or until soft.

Stir in the coriander and parsley, then serve with lemon wedges, dates and Moroccan or other crusty bread.

COOK'S TIP *The flavours of this soup develop on keeping. Use any very small pasta shapes if you don't have vermicelli.*

tunisian red pepper dip

felfal mathunn

This glorious, vibrant red dip catches the eye. It can be served with eggs, bread, olives and a little extra salad such as the one with cucumber and spring onion (*see page 143*) to make quite a substantial snack. Alternatively, try it as a small course on its own.

SERVES 4–6

3 large red peppers
1 red chilli
3–4 garlic cloves
3 tomatoes
2–3 tbsp olive oil
1 tsp caraway seeds
salt
2–3 eggs, hard boiled and sliced
125g (4oz) black olives, pitted

1 Grill the peppers, chilli, garlic and tomatoes until the skins are charred and blistered and all the vegetables are softened. During the grilling, turn over the vegetables once or twice so that they cook evenly. The peppers in particular will yield some juice, so choose a flameproof plate with a rim to catch any juice during grilling. Leave to cool slightly then peel the peppers and remove the core and the seeds. Skin the tomatoes and remove the seeds. Squeeze the garlic cloves so that the flesh comes away from the skin and deseed the chilli.

2 Put all the vegetables into a blender or food processor and process until almost smooth.

3 In a small frying pan, heat the oil and briefly fry the caraway seeds until fragrant. Stir into the vegetable purée and blend again. Season to taste, spoon into a bowl and chill before serving.

4 Serve in a bowl with pitta bread or Moroccan flat bread, hard-boiled eggs and black olives.

yellow lentil dip

bisir

This soft lentil purée has a soup-like consistency and robust character. It is delicious served with harissa and bread.

SERVES 4–6

250g (8oz) yellow or red lentils, rinsed
1–2 cloves garlic, finely chopped
3 tbsp olive oil
salt
black pepper
1 tsp cumin seeds, plus extra for garnish
½ tsp paprika, to garnish

TO SERVE

1 green cabbage, shredded
bread
harissa sauce (*see page 125*)

1 In a large pan, bring the lentils to the boil in double their volume of water and cook for 15 minutes then beat them well, add more water and cook again, skimming off the froth and beating several times until they form a very smooth, soft purée.

2 Beat in the garlic, 2 tablespoons olive oil and season to taste.

3 In a frying pan, heat the remaining olive oil and briefly fry the cumin seeds until lightly toasted and aromatic. Stir into the lentil purée.

4 Serve in a large dish with extra cumin and the paprika as a garnish.

5 Steam some shredded cabbage and serve on the side with a bowl of harissa and bread.

6 The traditional way to eat this dish is to dip the bread into the harissa and then into the bisir.

COOK'S TIP *Prepare this dip well in advance for the flavours to have plenty of time to develop.*

potato and olive tagine with preserved lemons

tagine batata

This hearty, spicy stew with floury potatoes is complemented by fresh sharp olives and silky preserved lemons. Look for really good green fleshy olives. Serve this with bread and the carrot and beetroot salad on page 140.

SERVES 4–6

- 2 tbsp olive oil
- 1 onion, finely chopped
- 2 cloves garlic, crushed
- 2 leeks, cleaned and chopped
- 2 tsp ground cumin
- ½ tsp curry powder
- 1 tsp freshly ground black pepper
- 2 red peppers, deseeded and sliced thinly
- 450g (1lb) potatoes, peeled and chopped
- 400g (14oz) can chopped tomatoes
- 1 tbsp tomato puree
- 75g (3oz) green olives, pitted
- 2–3 tbsp finely chopped fresh coriander
- 2–3 tbsp finely chopped fresh parsley
- preserved lemon

1 Heat the oil and cook the onion until translucent, then add the garlic and leeks and cook for a few minutes longer.

2 Add the spices and black pepper and stir well.

3 Add the peppers and potatoes and mix well into the cooked onion and the spices.

4 Pour over the tomatoes and stir in the tomato purée and green olives. Bring the mixture to the boil, adding a little water if the sauce is too thick.

5 Simmer for 30 minutes, stirring occasionally.

6 Adjust the seasoning and just before serving stir in the coriander and parsley and a few quarters of preserved lemon.

COOK'S TIP *Black pepper is a powerful spice. Add a smaller quantity if you prepfer a milder taste.*

egg and tomato tagine

bida maadesha

I had always associated tagines with slow, lengthy cooking but this is far from true. This delicious dish is made in a matter of minutes and provides a colourful, tasty supper. I have suggested one egg per person, for a more substantial dish put in two eggs each and use a larger pan.

SERVES 4

3–4 tbsp olive oil (or oil and butter mixed)
1 clove garlic, finely chopped
2–3 tbsp finely chopped fresh coriander
2–3 tbsp finely chopped fresh parsley
900g (2lb) tomatoes, quartered
1 tsp ground cumin
1 tsp paprika
1 tsp black pepper
1 whole chilli, optional
salt
4 eggs

1 Heat the oil or oil and butter mixture and gently fry the garlic, coriander and parsley.

2 Add the quartered tomatoes and mix. Add the cumin, paprika and black pepper. Add the whole chilli if you wish.

3 Mix well and then season with salt, cover the pan and cook for 5 minutes.

4 Uncover and stir, then break in the eggs and cook gently for 5–6 minutes so that the whites cook and the yolks set.

5 Serve hot straight from the pan.

COOK'S TIP *Leave the chilli whole, as it makes it easier to spot and remove before serving.*

bean and spinach tagine

tagine loubya

This is a great way to combine spinach, tomatoes and beans. I prefer to use larger haricot beans as you get more bean and less skin! You can use lima beans or small butter beans instead. If you are in a hurry, cook the beans first and then add them to the rest of the ingredients (with their cooking water) but leave enough time for the sauce to heat through and for the beans to absorb the flavours. As with many dishes like this, the flavours develop if the tagine is left to stand.

SERVES 4

2 tbsp olive oil
1 large onion, finely chopped
2 cloves garlic, crushed
2 large spring onions, finely chopped
125g (4oz) dried haricot beans (or lima, cannelini or butter beans) soaked overnight
2–3 tsp paprika
1 tsp ground cumin
400ml (12fl oz) water or stock
1 chilli, deseeded and chopped
400g (14oz) can chopped tomatoes
1 tbsp tomato purée
125–175g (4–6oz) spinach
salt and pepper

1 In a large flame- and ovenproof casserole or tagine, heat the oil and fry the onion, garlic and spring onions until soft.

2 Add the uncooked beans and spices and cook for a few minutes, then add 400ml (12fl oz) water or vegetable stock. Bring to the boil and boil fiercely for 10 minutes then add the chilli, tomatoes, tomato purée. Bring to the boil, cover the pan and cook in the oven, or over a low heat, for 45–60 minutes or until the beans are quite soft.

3 If necessary, reduce the liquid by stirring the mixture over a high heat for a few minutes.

4 Just before serving, add the spinach, mix well and cook for 3–4 minutes.

5 Season to taste and serve with bread.

couscous with chickpeas and vegetables

khundar couscous

This dish looks and sounds elaborate but is actually really easy to make either for a simple supper or dressed up with extras for a party. Couscous is a light tasty grain and is delicious if steamed twice. Don't be put off by this as the first steaming can be done well ahead and the second steaming warms the couscous through and the grain is then very light in texture. Couscous can be varied according to the vegetables on hand, what you do need though is plenty of sauce.

SERVES 4–6

400g (14oz) couscous
1 tbsp olive oil

FOR THE SAUCE
2 tbsp olive oil
1 onion, chopped
1 leek, cleaned and chopped
4 spring onions, chopped
2 cloves garlic
1 tsp cumin seed
1 tsp coriander seed
1 cinnamon stick
2–3 tbsp finely chopped coriander
2–3 tbsp finely chopped parsley
2 carrots, peeled and diced
2 turnips, scrubbed and diced
1 aubergine, cubed
125g (4oz) cooked weight chickpeas or lentils
400g (14oz) can chopped tomatoes
300ml (10fl oz) vegetable stock
salt and black pepper

TO SERVE
whole roasted tomatoes, shallots and/or steamed cabbage wedges

1 Rinse the couscous in several changes of water until clear as this removes the starch, then pour the couscous into a steamer forming a mound. The bottom of the steamer or sieve should not be touching the water. Steam for about 6–8 minutes. Do not cover, eventually the steam should come out in a column from the top of the mound (as long as your steamer components fit tightly together). Otherwise check that the grain has swelled.

2 Remove from the heat and tip on a plate and sprinkle with cold water and some salt. Separate the grains and leave to cool. Add the olive oil and work through the couscous using your hands to break up all the lumps and separate the grains. Set aside.

3 For the sauce, heat the oil and fry the onion, leek and spring onions. Add the garlic, cumin, coriander seed, cinnamon and season with black pepper and salt.

4 Add the fresh herbs, carrots, turnips, aubergine and chickpeas. Mix well and pour over the tomatoes and stock. Bring to the boil and simmer for 30 minutes.

5 Just before serving, steam the couscous again for 6–8 minutes.

6 Pile the hot couscous round a large plate or bowl and leave a space in the centre. Put the cooked vegetables in the middle and use the sauce to moisten the grain.

7 For a party dish, decorate with whole roasted tomatoes, shallots and/or quarters of cooked cabbage.

TIMESAVER *The first steaming of the couscous can be done in advance.*

carrot and beetroot salad

shlada

Try to get really well-flavoured carrots for this glorious, colourful salad. If they are young and slender you will need more but avoid any that are too big as the centre may be woody.

SERVES 4

6–10 carrots
2 beetroots
1 tbsp olive oil
2 cloves garlic, finely chopped
2 tsp cumin seeds
1 tsp paprika
1 tsp black pepper
salt

1 Peel the carrots if necessary and then boil whole until tender. When cool, cut into neat dice.

2 Cook the beetroots in their skins in a separate saucepan for about 25 minutes or until tender. Leave to cool, peel and cut into neat dice.

3 Heat the oil in a large frying pan and fry the garlic slowly so that it does not brown, then add the cumin seed and paprika and mix in. Add the diced carrot and beetroot, sauté briskly in the oil and spice mixture. Season to taste with salt.

4 Serve warm or cold.

spiced cabbage with raisins

kromb

This dish can be eaten as a side vegetable or used to garnish couscous. To ring the changes, use slivers of apricots instead of raisins.

SERVES 4

- 25g (1oz) butter or butter and oil mixed
- 1 clove garlic, finely chopped
- 450g (1lb) green or white compact cabbage, shredded
- 50g (2oz) raisins
- 1 tsp coriander seed
- 1 tbsp tomato purée
- salt and black pepper
- 2 tbsp finely chopped parsley
- 2 tbsp finely chopped coriander

1 Heat the butter or butter and oil mixture and cook the garlic briefly over a low heat so it does not scorch.

2 Add the cabbage to the pan and cook gently so that it softens. Add the raisins and mix well.

3 Dry roast the coriander seed until lightly toasted and then crush in a pestle and mortar.

4 Mix the coriander seed into the cabbage and add the tomato purée mixed with 3–4 tablespoons water.

5 Simmer until the cabbage is cooked and the water evaporated.

6 Season to taste. Just before serving mix in the chopped fresh herbs.

aubergine and mixed pepper salad

dbenjal meshwe

This is another simple, well-flavoured salad, showing the versatility of the aubergine. Steaming it first means that you don't need so much oil, which keeps the salad light. You can mash the aubergine slightly when cooking it with the spice mixture which helps the flavours permeate the dish. Yellow and red peppers are easier to skin than green and may cook a little bit quicker.

SERVES 4

1 aubergine
3 peppers, (red, yellow, green)
3–4 tbsp olive oil
1 clove garlic, finely chopped
1 tsp cumin seed
1/4 tsp dried chilli flakes
1–2 tbsp fresh coriander, roughly chopped
salt and pepper

1 Cut the stalk end off the aubergine and cut into bite-size cubes. Then steam until soft.

2 Roast the peppers until the skin is charred. Put in a plastic bag to cool slightly then peel the skins and remove the seeds. Chop into bite-size chunks.

3 Heat the oil in a frying pan, cook the garlic slowly so it does not brown and become bitter. Add the spices and cook for about 5 minutes.

4 Add the prepared peppers and aubergine and mix together for the flavours to develop.

5 Season well and leave to cool, then serve with fresh coriander.

cucumber, spring onion, tomato and green olive salad

kherya shlada

This is a refreshing, colourful mixture with the olives adding a clean piquant taste. Serve the salad with bread and salty cheese or just use with many of the other small mezze dishes from the Mediterranean rim. Use fat, fleshy green olives. It is probably best to buy these whole and remove the stones yourself.

SERVES 4

1 cucumber
3 spring onions
4 fresh tomatoes
125g (4oz) green olives, chopped
1 tsp lemon juice
2 tbsp olive oil
1 tsp mild vinegar
salt and black pepper

1 Chop the cucumber and spring onions very finely.

2 Skin the tomatoes and chop finely.

3 In a large bowl, mix these ingredients together with the green olives.

4 Make a dressing with the lemon juice, olive oil, and vinegar. Season well and toss into the salad.

moroccan flat bread

khobs

Bread is an absolute staple of the Moroccan diet and is eaten at or with virtually every meal except couscous. Families will make their own bread from start to finish or sometimes make just the dough and take it along to the local bakery to be finished off. The breads are generally flat and can be flavoured with sesame seeds and aniseeds.

MAKES 2 LOAVES

675g (1½lb) strong white flour
1 sachet dried yeast
1 tsp salt
1 tbsp olive oil
375–400ml (13–14fl oz) warm water
olive oil for brushing

1 In a large bowl mix the flour, yeast and salt. Work the oil well through the flour then pour over most of the warm water and draw the mixture up to a dough. It will be very sticky at first but do not be tempted to add extra flour. Knead the dough well by stretching it firmly across a work surface and then fold back in. Once it begins to feel less sticky add more water and then knead to work well in. The dough needs to be very soft and flexible.

2 Leave the dough to rise in a warm place for about 15–30 minutes in a clean bowl covered with a cloth.

3 Divide in two and knead each piece again and shape into a ball.

4 Flatten each ball into a round and leave to rise on a cloth in a warm place.

5 Once the dough has risen, flip off the cloth onto a baking tray and prick right through in 5 or 6 places.

6 Bake at 200°C (400°F) Gas Mark 6 for about 30 minutes. Cool on a wire rack and brush with olive oil while still warm.

moroccan flaky pastries

raaiff

These are not tricky but do need practising to get the consistency right. Fatima, who showed me how to make them, has made bread in the mornings since she was a child. In many Moroccan families this is the way great cooking traditions are passed on. The cheese-filled raaiff make a tasty savoury to eat with salad or as a snack; plain ones are eaten with butter and honey or fruit preserves.

MAKES 7–8

300g (10oz) strong white flour
1/4 tsp salt
50g (2oz) butter
1 tbsp oil
100–125ml (3½–4fl oz) warm water
extra oil for coating the dough balls and oiling the tray
up to 125g (4oz) grated hard cheese

1 Put the flour and salt into a large bowl and rub in the butter until it is evenly distributed. Work in the oil and then pour over most of the warm water.

2 Knead the dough by stretching it firmly across the work surface adding more water to get a very soft consistency. Work the dough until it is soft and very elastic; as you knead you should hear air bubbles popping in the dough.

3 Divide the dough into 7–8 balls by squeezing pieces out between your thumb and finger. Place the balls on a well-oiled tray or earthenware dish, brush with oil, cover with a cloth, and leave for 15–20 minutes.

4 Take each ball and pat out into a small circle on an oiled surface, then turn over and pat out again. Repeat this process until you have a dinner-plate size piece of dough. Oil your finger tips and then start to pull the dough out very thinly using your thumb and forefinger, trying not to tear it in the process (this is the part that takes a bit of practice). Work around the dough pulling the edges further each time. Once the edges are pulled out, oil your hands again, lift the dough away from the work surface, placing your whole hand underneath to support the very thin (almost membrane-like) dough and flap slightly to get air underneath to stretch out the centre part. The final result should be a large rough rectangle. Do not worry too much about the holes, they are almost inevitable and won't matter once the dough is folded.

5 For cheese raaiff, fold in one long edge and scatter with grated cheese, then fold over the other long edge to cover the cheese, then fold in the short ends to overlap in the middle.

6 For plain raaiff do the same but leave out the cheese.

7 Heat a heavy frying pan or griddle until very hot and then cook the raaiff individually for several minutes until well browned and puffed. Plain raaiff are better drizzled with a little oil as they cook.

orange and apricots with cinnamon

lechein mishmesh masel

This colourful, refreshing fruit dish is served with savoury tagines or as a dessert. If there is any left over chill it and have it for breakfast. Buy really good-quality apricots and large juicy oranges for this recipe.

SERVES 4

2 oranges
200g (7oz) whole dried apricots
2 tbsp caster sugar
200ml (7fl oz) water
1 large cinnamon stick

1 Using a serrated knife or a very sharp knife for a smoother finish, slice the peel away from either end of the oranges, exposing the flesh. Stand the fruit upright and cut away the peel and pith in sections following the curve of the fruit. Working over a plate or a bowl to catch the juice, hold the orange in one hand and cut down either side of the membrane and then remove the neat orange segments.

2 Put the segments in a pan with any juice, then add the apricots, sugar, water and cinnamon stick, broken in half.

3 Bring to the boil, then cover the pan and simmer for 30–35 minutes or until the apricots are very plump and soft.

4 Chill well before serving.

COOK'S TIP *The cinnamon bark adds a lovely warm flavour and can be left in or removed before serving.*

india

Indian food is a vegetarian's treasure trove and its range of flavours, from subtle to intense, is as vast as the land itself.

Indian food is not one cuisine, but a whole medley of cooking styles from many differing regions. Climate and geography, from the low-lying coasts to the mountainous interior, play a part in influencing local dishes. Invaders, conquerors, explorers and traders have all influenced the food in this huge subcontinent, importing ideas as well as ingredients.The recipes in this chapter have been given to me by friends and family throughout India, and range from mildly flavoured coconut rice to hot biryani and spicy potatoes. I have had great fun trying the different flavours and ways of working with spices and I hope you will be equally tempted. Most of the recipes can be varied, depending on what you have to hand. The sambal dressing on page 178, for example, is a gorgeous mellow mix of coconut with a hint of ginger and chilli. It is delicious with mangetout or sugar-snap peas, but would be equally good with many other vegetables.

Rice, pulses, bread, vegetables and nuts with a few dairy products form the backbone of the diet, yet I am struck by the regional versatility using just these few ingredients. Rice, for example, a staple for a large part of India, particularly the south, can be served plain or seasoned with spices, either hot or aromatic. The spiced biryani (*page 173*) is a typical dish from Hyderabad. In this sumptuous mélange the rice is coloured with saffron, enriched with yogurt, almonds and cashews and spiced with ginger and chillies. In contrast, coconut rice (*page 162*) is mildly flavoured with cinnamon, cardamom and cloves, and enriched with coconut milk, a widely used ingredient in the tropical south. Different again is kitchuri, a dish from Calcutta where the rice is cooked with split peas or lentils, giving it a pleasant light texture. Rice and split peas need to be on hand for the monsoon period because the heavy Calcutta rains can make it impossible to shop at times. It is no surprise that recipes from these parts can be made from store-cupboard standbys.

the spice continent

What really gives so much Indian cooking a distinctive note is the ingenious and varying use of spices, a vital thread running throughout this vast subcontinent. In Indian cookery, spices have many functions beyond flavouring: some colour, some thicken; sometimes they add heat or a cooling note; some help digestion or cleanse the palate. Spices may be used fresh or dried, as even that process can change the flavour. They can be used whole or ground (a pestle and mortar is a standard piece of kitchen equipment).

During the cooking process spices are treated quite differently to produce varied effects. Most common is probably the spice paste, similar to spice pastes of Asia, which I've used in recipes such as stuffed aubergines and sambal dressing (*pages 163* and *178* respectively). A simple mix is made of onion, garlic and ginger with coriander, cumin and chillies added according to taste.

Roasting and frying spices brings out a different flavour. This can be done at the start of the recipe, as in coconut rice, but it is also done to create a last-minute seasoning called a *tarka*, which I have found a really useful idea.

individual herbs and spices

It is best to buy spices whole as they retain their flavour and potency for much longer. Keep spices in airtight containers in a cool dry place. Spice mixtures, once made, will keep for two or three months, but the sooner you use them the better. Be ruthless about throwing away old spices!

spice pastes

Garlic, ginger and onions are often mashed to a paste before being cooked. These pastes would traditionally have been ground or mashed by hand, but modern food processors are a real boon, making this job simple and quick. If you don't have one, though, finely chop everything by hand, then finish the mashing with a pestle and mortar.

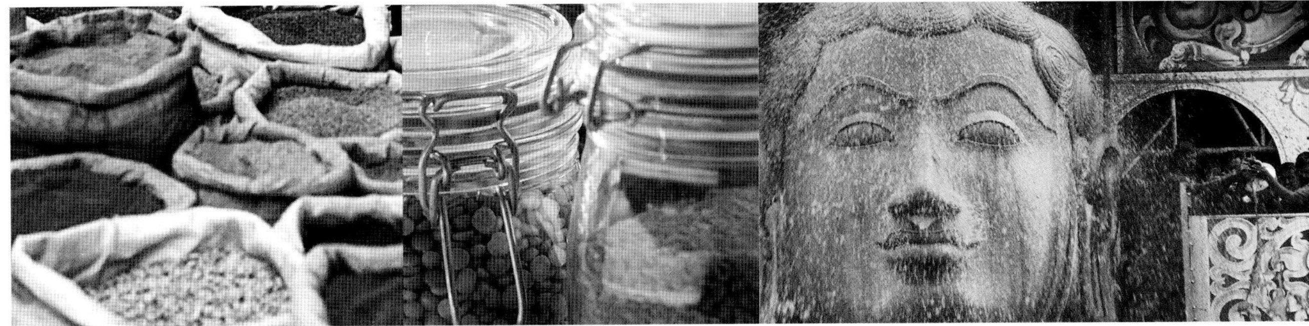

While many of us can hold in our minds the taste of a single spice and use it confidently, an Indian cook may choose from some 25 or so spices to make a *masala* or combination. A great deal of care and thought goes into the preparation of a spice blend and it is rather like the cookery equivalent of an artist mixing paints on a palette. There are several classic spice blends which it is worth trying to make yourself and, as you get more confident, you can alter them to suit your own taste preferences.

Garam masala is one of the commonest spice mixtures used in Indian cooking. In fact, literally translated, *masala* means mixture. A variety of spices such as cinnamon, cloves and black pepper may make the basic mixture. Sometimes nutmeg, ground bay leaves, coriander and cumin are added, which impart a more distinctive aroma and taste to the food. Many families have their own recipes for these blends; the friend who gave me the recipe for stuffed aubergines (*page 163*) still has her mother send her the family *garam masala*, despite having lived in England for 20 years.

Panch phoron is a mixture originating from Bengal. The spices are used whole and consist of roughly equal quantities of cumin, fennel seed, fenugreek, mustard and nigella. This combination produces an aromatic rather than hot mix and it is worth frying and stirring it into vegetables.

In the south of India, vegetable and lentil dishes are often flavoured with a mix called *sambaar podi* or *sambaar* powder. It is a hot spicy mixture that makes you sweat, which then helps you cool down. The spices used in the *sambal* give you a taste of this – chillies, ginger, cumin seed and turmeric. A *sambal podi* (it can also be called *sambaar podi*) usually also contains black pepper, coriander and different varieties of ground pulses.

common ingredients and useful techniques

cardamom

An aromatic spice from south-western India. Black cardamom seeds are contained in small green pods about the size of a large lemon pip. The spice has a pungent aroma and a warm, spicy-sweet flavour. Cardamom can be bought in the pod or ground, but the ground seeds soon lose their flavour. To grind your own seeds, remove from the pod and crush in a pestle and mortar. If using cardamom to flavour dishes such as stews and curries, lightly crush the whole pod or slit it open and add it to the mixture: the shell will disintegrate while the dish cooks. The seeds of cardamom are also infused in milk to flavour desserts, including *kulfi* (Indian ice cream) and creamy rice puddings.

coriander and mint

These fresh herbs are used in Indian cooking and have the effect of cooling down some of the hot ingredients.

ginger

The fresh root is widely used and is most often made into a pulp with garlic and onions and cooked at the beginning of a recipe.

chilli

The spicy curries of Indian cuisine are flavoured by hot fiery red and green chillies. Red chillies can be dried, ground and added with other spices, or simply cut lengthways to flavour food and then easily removed before serving.

mustard seeds

These little reddish-brown seeds are used more often in southern and eastern Indian cooking. They are frequently infused in oil and add a lively flavour.

tamarind

Adds a sharp sour flavour to much southern Indian food. Look for ready-made tamarind paste, which is extremely convenient to use.

saffron

This spice was brought to India by the Persians and is used to colour and flavour sweet and savoury dishes. It imparts a glorious colour to rice, such as in biryani, but also flavours the delicate custard in *phirni* (*page 183*).

grinding spices

For small amounts of spice it makes sense to use a pestle and mortar. Larger quantities can be ground in a spice mill. A small electric coffee grinder is fine, but it is best to keep one just for this purpose if you can.

dry roasting

Use a heavy frying pan to roast whole spices for a minute or two, keeping a close watch so they don't burn. As they cook they will release a fragrance.

frying spices

Infusing spices in hot oil releases their flavour. Add whole spices first and be careful not to burn them. They puff up and brown very quickly and the seeds should pop. When frying ground spices, lower the heat or they will scorch.

paneer (panir)

Paneer is a fresh cheese made from the curds of cow's milk. It is usually cubed, then cooked with vegetables.

yogurt

A couple of the recipes are cooked with yogurt. It is best to use a full-fat yogurt as it is less likely to curdle. Beating the yogurt well before adding it also helps to stabilize it.

ghee

Ghee is simply butter which has been clarified to remove all the milk solids, so that you may even deep-fry in it. If you cannot buy ready-made ghee, make your own. Put 250g (8oz) unsalted butter in a small, heavy pan and melt over a low heat. Simmer very gently for about 45 minutes without stirring, until the milk solids turn brown. Turn off the heat and let the solids settle, then strain the ghee through double muslin. Store in the refrigerator.

vegetable pakora with mint chutney and fresh tomato chutney

These hot and satisfying vegetable fritters are served with a mint chutney. Eaten with a cup of spiced India tea – *chai* – they are a perfect teatime snack. Known in the West variously as *ajowan*, *ajwain* or *carom*, these seeds, which have a slight thyme or caraway flavour, are often added to the batter of this dish in India. Use these if you wish or a mixture of dried thyme and oregano.

vegetable pakora

SERVES 4–6

150g (5oz) cauliflower florets
2 onions
1 small aubergine
75g (3oz) spinach
oil to deep-fry

THE BATTER
250g (8oz) (besan) gram flour
½-1 tsp salt
⅓ tsp bicarbonate of soda
2 tsp ajwain (carom) seeds or 1 tsp dried thyme and 1 tsp dried oregano
1 tsp red chilli powder

1 Prepare the vegetables: Wash the cauliflower florets. Slice the onions thinly. Cut the aubergines into ½-cm (¼-inch) slices. Cut the stems off the spinach leaves.

2 For the batter: sieve the gram flour, salt and bicarbonate of soda together. Add ajwain seeds or dried thyme and oregano, red chilli powder and 250ml (8fl oz) water to make a batter.

3 Heat oil to smoking point and reduce to medium heat. Dip vegetables in the batter and deep-fry until golden brown and crisp.

mint chutney

50g (2oz) mint leaves, stalks removed
1 tsp lemon juice or more to taste
½ tsp sugar
salt to taste
(½ cup chopped raw green mango can also be added)

1 To make the chutney, use a food processor or blender and grind the ingredients together with a little water to make a thick paste.

fresh tomato chutney

4 fresh tomatoes
1 onion
1 clove garlic
1 chilli
¼ tsp salt
¼ tsp sugar

1 Pierce the skin of the tomatoes and place in a large bowl and cover with boiling water. Leave for 3–4 minutes then remove with a slotted spoon and peel off the skins.

2 Process the onion, garlic and chilli in a blender or food processor, add the tomatoes and process until fairly smooth. Add salt and sugar to taste.

samosas with spiced yogurt

These little parcels filled with a traditional spiced mixture of beans and potato are very easy to make with filo pastry. They can then be baked rather than deep fried. If you cut down on the spices, they make a great snack for children, served hot or cold.

samosas

MAKES 16

450g (1lb) potatoes
150g (5oz) green beans
2 tbsp oil
1 onion, chopped
4 cloves garlic
2 tsp cumin seed
1 or 2 green chillies, deseeded and diced
½ tsp turmeric
2 tbsp fresh coriander, chopped
16 sheets filo pastry
vegetable oil

1 Peel the potatoes and boil until tender. Cut into small cubes or mash very roughly.

2 Trim the beans and steam until just tender, then chop finely.

In a medium pan, heat the oil and fry the onion with the garlic, cumin and chillies until golden. Stir in the turmeric powder

3 Add the cooked potato and beans and the fresh coriander. Mix well and season to taste.

4 Using a whole sheet of filo folded in half lengthways, or a half sheet for a thinner wrap, brush the sheet well with oil, then put a tablespoon of filling at one end. Wrap the pastry around the filling by folding it over in neat triangles.

5 Brush well with oil.

6 Bake at 200°C (400°F) Gas Mark 6 for 15–20 minutes. Serve with some spiced yogurt (see below).

spiced yogurt

raita

1 tbsp sunflower oil
2–3 curry leaves
½ tsp cumin seed
¼ tsp turmeric
300g (10oz) thick yogurt

1 Heat the oil and fry the curry leaves and cumin until very lightly toasted, add a little turmeric.

2 Remove the pan from the heat and leave to cool.

3 Stir in yogurt and season to taste.

dal

Dal is the general term for pulses – dried beans, peas and lentils – which are cooked on almost a daily basis in many Indian homes. The name is also given to many dishes using these ingredients.

In some areas the extensive use of pulses makes up for the relative lack of fresh vegetables. Each region has its own favourite recipes and cooking methods vary, though on the whole dals are well seasoned with spices to counteract their fairly bland earthy flavour.

Sometimes the pulses are simply boiled in water and, once cooked, mashed with herbs and spices. Dal can also be steamed with flavourings so that the resulting purée is quite dry, or cooked with rice to produce quite a different texture. Once cooked, dal is sometimes seasoned with a spiced infused oil.

Many spices are used to flavour dal. Turmeric is popular and adds a warming golden hue. Lightly roasted coriander and cumin seeds are frequently used to give flavour and aid digestion. Pungent garlic and clean-tasting ginger are often made into a paste, fried, then stirred in. There can be chillies (whole or ground), curry leaves, mustard seeds, fried onion and tomatoes. A finished dal may be anything from spicy-sweet to scorching hot; the texture can be liquid almost to the point of soup, or quite creamy and thick or dry.

Whole pulses need to be soaked overnight. Drain, cover in cold water, bring to the boil, keep at full boil for 10 minutes, then simmer briskly until soft (cooking times will vary). Skim off any scum that rises to the surface. Don't add salt to the cooking water as this hardens the beans. Once cooked, drain the beans (reserve the liquor for stock) and use as required.

Split peas and lentils can be cooked without soaking, but cook more quickly if soaked for an hour or so. Drain, cover with cold water, and bring them to the boil, but there is no need for prolonged boiling. Watch carefully, as they have a tendency to boil over.

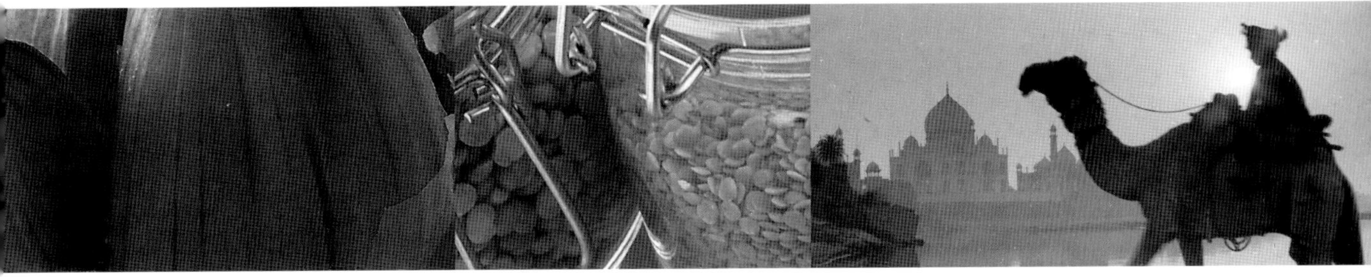

whole beans

chickpeas

Found frequently in Indian food, chickpeas are round and knobbly in shape and pale golden brown in colour. Dried chickpeas must always be soaked overnight prior to cooking. Once cooked, they retain their shape and colour well. In India they are often cooked whole and seasoned and served as snacks. Chickpeas are also ground into a creamy fine golden flour, which is used for making pakora and bhajis. The Indian name for the chickpea is *chana*, which is also used for small yellow split peas.

black-eye beans

Black-eye beans are fairly small, kidney-shaped and cream-coloured with a black spot or eye. They are one of the quicker cooking pulses with a savoury, slightly smoky flavour. *Chora dal* is the name for split black-eye beans.

red kidney beans

Red kidney beans, also called *rajma*, are popular in Punjabi cookery.

split peas and lentils

Any specialist Indian shop has an astounding range of split peas and small lentils on offer, and the numerous varieties can all be prepared in many different ways. Generally they should be bought split and skinned because, when the skin is left on, the purée tends to be rather dull in colour and the texture is coarser.

chana dal

These are very like small yellow split peas. They are also ground very finely and used in spice mixtures.

masoor dal

A pinky-red split pea, very similar to a red lentil.

moong dal

These are tiny green beans sometimes called mung beans. When split and skinned they are yellow and have a more delicate texture than yellow split peas.

urad dal

These are ivory white seeds from the hulled and split black gram bean, which are popular in northern India and make a creamy white purée.

fragrant coconut rice

tenkaya annamu

This is a tasty versatile rice dish fragrant with cinnamon, cloves and cardamom. It is delicious served with the stuffed aubergines (on the page opposite) but is also excellent with many other spiced dishes.

SERVES 4

400g (14oz) basmati rice
2 tbsp sunflower or vegetable oil
1 onion, finely chopped
1 green chilli, cut lengthways
4 small sticks cinnamon
8 cloves
6 cardamom pods
4–6 tbsp finely chopped fresh coriander
3–4 tbsp finely chopped mint
1 litre ($1\frac{3}{4}$ pints) coconut milk
½ tsp salt

1 Wash the rice in a sieve and then soak for 30 minutes in a large bowl of cold water.

2 In a heavy bottomed pan or flameproof casserole, heat the oil and fry the onion with the green chilli. Add the cinnamon sticks and cloves. Slit the tops of the cardamom pods and add to the pan.

3 Cook the mixture over a low heat for several minutes for the spices to infuse, then add the coriander and mint.

4 Fry everything together then add the drained rice, coconut milk and salt. Bring to the boil and simmer for 30 minutes or until the rice is tender and the liquid absorbed.

stuffed aubergines

nune vankaya

For this dish you need the small egg-size aubergines, which are available in specialist shops and occasionally in the bigger supermarkets. This is a very thick curry and quite difficult to stir but try to turn the aubergines over without breaking them up. The many ready-made garam masalas available do vary, so try several to find your own favourite.

SERVES 4

1 whole head of garlic
2.5-cm (1-inch) fresh root ginger, grated
2–3 tsp garam masala
½ tsp turmeric
4 tbsp oil
6–8 small egg-size aubergines
1 tsp cumin seed
227g (8oz) can chopped tomatoes
½ tsp tamarind pulp
salt

1 Peel all the garlic cloves and crush with the grated ginger to make a spice paste. Divide in half.

2 Mix one half of the ginger–garlic mixture with 2–3 teaspoons of garam masala, turmeric and salt,

3 Trim the tops off the aubergines and cut down ⅔ of the length into quarters. It is important not to cut all the way through as the aubergine quarters need to stay together.

4 Fill the aubergines with the ginger–garlic and turmeric mixture, then press back into shape.

5 In a large frying pan, heat 3 tablespoons of oil and fry the aubergines until browned, turning over carefully to ensure even cooking. Set aside.

6 In a separate pan (big enough to hold the aubergines), heat 1 tablespoon of oil and fry the onion. Add the remaining garlic and ginger mixture, the cumin seed and cook for a few minutes, then add the tomatoes and tamarind pulp and cook for a few minutes or until the smell of the tomatoes disappears.

7 Add the partially cooked aubergines and cover the pan. Cook very gently for 15–20 minutes. Season to taste and serve hot.

green curry with coconut

korma

The 'greenness' of this curry comes more from the fresh herbs than the vegetables. It is delicious with plain rice and a choice of raita or chutney. The vegetables I have suggested make a good combination but can be varied according to the season.

SERVES 4

1 tbsp coriander seed
6 cloves garlic, crushed
1-cm (1/2-inch) fresh ginger root, grated
1 green chilli, deseeded and finely chopped
4 tbsp sunflower oil
1/2 tsp cumin seed
1/2 tsp turmeric
1 small head cauliflower approx. 400g (14oz)
250g (8oz) green beans
2 medium-size potatoes
1 onion, chopped
100ml (3 1/2fl oz) coconut milk
1 tbsp finely chopped fresh mint
3 tbsp finely chopped fresh coriander
2 tbsp lemon juice

1 Roast the coriander seed in a dry frying pan, then cool and grind finely in a pestle and mortar or spice mill.

2 Prepare the garlic, ginger and chilli and mix together to make a pulp. Process in a spice mill if necessary to make smooth.

3 In a large frying pan, heat the oil and fry the cumin seed, add the garlic and ginger pulp and turmeric. Add the ground coriander and cook for a few minutes or until the smell has gone from the coriander.

4 Mix in all the vegetables, cut into quite small pieces.

5 Add the coconut milk with the chopped fresh mint and coriander.

6 Add a little water and cook very gently until tender.

7 Remove the pan from the heat and add lemon juice to taste. Serve hot.

TIMESAVER *The coriander can be roasted and ground in advance. Make the garlic and ginger spice pulp ahead of time, too.*

lentils with tarka

tarka dal

In the predominantly vegetarian cuisine of southern India, many lentil and vegetable dishes are flavoured with *tarka*. This is a fragrant butter prepared by frying various spices in hot ghee or oil. The flavours are released in seconds and the aromatic mixture is immediately stirred into the cooked lentils.

SERVES 4

125g (4oz) red lentils
2 tbsp oil
2.5-cm (1-inch) fresh ginger root, grated
2 cloves garlic crushed
½ tsp turmeric
1 chilli, deseeded and chopped
2 tsp ground coriander
1 onion, chopped
1 carrot, chopped
1 potato, diced
1 tbsp tamarind pulp
small handful coriander leaves
salt

FOR THE TARKA

2 tbsp ghee or vegetable oil
½ tsp black mustard seed
3 dried chillies
2–3 curry leaves

1 Rinse the lentils and leave to drain.

2 In a heavy bottomed pan, heat the oil and fry the spices, then add the onion and fry until translucent.

3 Add the lentils to the pan with 600ml (1 pint) water and bring the mixture to the boil.

4 Add the vegetables and bring to the boil, then cover the pan and simmer until everything is soft.

5 When soft, remove the lid and cook for 5–10 minutes to reduce the liquid and thicken the mixture.

6 Add the tamarind and coriander leaves, reserving some for garnish. In a separate small pan, heat the ghee or oil and fry the mustard seed, chillies and curry leaves.

7 Just heat through until the mustard seeds pop and then pour the mixture over the lentils. Serve garnished with the remaining coriander leaves.

TIMESAVER *Soaking the lentils for 30 minutes or so will make them quicker to cook.*

chickpea curry with ginger

chana fabji

Chickpeas are popular in many Indian recipes. Roasted dried chickpeas are frequently sold in the street markets as snacks and chickpea flour is used for breads and batters. In curries they are also useful as they have a full nutty flavour and hold their shape well when cooked which makes a good contrast to the many split pulses that fall into a purée when cooked.

SERVES 4

250g (8oz) dried chickpeas, soaked overnight
2 medium onions, finely chopped
2 cloves garlic
2 tbsp grated fresh ginger root
1 tbsp ground coriander
1 tsp ground cardamom
½ tsp dried chilli flakes
4–6 tbsp sunflower oil
2 tomatoes, finely chopped
125–150ml (4–5fl oz) stock or liquid from cooking chickpeas
juice of 1 lemon
salt and pepper

1 Drain the chickpeas and cook in plenty of boiling water for 45–50 minutes or until soft. Drain and reserve the cooking liquid

2 Using a food processor or blender, process the onions, garlic, ginger, coriander, cardamom and chilli flakes to a paste adding a little water if necessary.

3 Heat the oil in a large frying pan and cook the paste for 10 minutes allowing to brown slightly.

4 Add the tomatoes and cook for a further 2–3 minutes.

5 Add the cooked chickpeas and stock, or the cooking liquid from the chickpeas, and lemon juice.

6 Bring the mixture to the boil and simmer uncovered for 20 minutes. Season well with salt and black pepper.

TIMESAVER *Remember to soak the chickpeas overnight. If you're really pushed for time, substitute canned ones which need no preparation.*

spiced rice and peas

kitchuri

Kitchuri can be made from basics and is very much a comfort food. Calcutta is often beset by monsoon floods, which make it impossible to shop. Most Bengalis associate *kitchuri* with this season, and keep its ingredients to hand. It's a kind of emergency meal – I've heard stories of intrepid adventurers ensuring they have rice and dal for wilderness treks. If any *kitchuri* remains, make an omelette, slice it and stir it with the leftovers for a nutritious snack.

SERVES 4

250g (8oz) basmati rice
125g (4oz) yellow moong dal
3 tbsp butter
1 onion chopped
1–2 cloves garlic, crushed
2.5-cm (1-inch) fresh ginger root, grated
4 cloves
1 cinnamon stick
6 cardamom pods
½ teaspoon peppercorns
¼ tsp turmeric powder
salt
150g (5oz) pickling onions

FOR THE GARNISH

crispy fried onions and/or coriander or parsley

1 Mix the rice and dal in a sieve, rinse well and then leave to soak in a large bowl while preparing the other ingredients.

2 In a large flameproof casserole, melt the butter and fry the onion and garlic until beginning to brown. Add the ginger and fry for a few minutes longer then add the remaining spices (except the turmeric) and cook for 1–2 minutes more.

3 Drain the rice and dal mixture and add to the frying mixture. Sprinkle on the turmeric and mix while continuing to fry.

4 Add boiling water to come 2-cm (¾-inch) above the rice and add salt. Cover the pan and simmer gently until the rice is cooked.

5 In the meantime, peel the pickling onions by immersing in boiling water for a few minutes. Repeat if difficult to peel. Then add the peeled onions to the pan so the onions cook in the mixture.

6 Adjust the seasoning to taste. Serve hot garnished with crispy fried onions and/or coriander or parsley,

hyderabadi biryani

This biryani is light but flavourful. My friend Mamta, who gave me the recipe, said that the smell was so tempting that the family could hardly wait for the biryani to be cooked!

SERVES 4

2–3 tsp garam masala (see below)
350g (12oz) basmati rice
salt
250ml (8 fl oz) yogurt
1 tsp saffron
2 tbsp milk, warmed
125g (4oz) ghee
100g (3½oz) onions, sliced
4 green chillies
2.5cm (1 inch) ginger, julienned
4 cloves garlic, finely chopped
½ tsp turmeric powder
1 tsp red chilli powder
500g (1¼ lb) mixed vegetables (potatoes, carrots, French beans), diced
50g (2oz) cashew nuts
50g (2oz) almonds, blanched and sliced
25g (1oz) mint leaves, finely chopped
25g (1oz) coriander, finely chopped

FOR THE GARAM MASALA
6 green cardamom pods
2 black cardamom pods
6 cloves
2 x 2½cm (1-inch) sticks cinnamon
2 bay leaves
pinch of mace

1 Preheat the oven to 190°C (375°F) Gas Mark 5. Grind together all the ingredients for the garam masala.

2 Wash the rice in running water and soak for 30 minutes. Drain, put in a large pan with 750ml (1¼ pints) fresh cold water. Add half the garam masala and the salt. Bring to the boil and boil for 5–8 minutes or until the rice is almost done. Drain, if necessary, and set aside.

3 In a small bowl, whisk the yogurt and divide into two equal portions.

4 Dissolve the saffron in the warm milk and stir into one portion of yogurt. Mix well and set aside.

5 Heat the ghee in a pan. Add the rest of garam masala and sauté over medium heat until it begins to crackle. Add the onions and sauté until golden brown, add the green chillies, ginger and garlic. Sauté for 1 minute then add the turmeric and red chilli powder and cook for a few seconds.

6 Stir in the diced vegetables, then the plain yogurt and 175 ml (6 fl oz) water. Bring to the boil, and simmer until the vegetables are cooked.

7 Remove from the heat and add the nuts. Season to taste.

8 Put in an ovenproof casserole and cover with the reserved saffron yogurt, the mint and coriander. Top with the rice. Cover tightly with foil and bake for 15–20 minutes at190°C (375°F) Gas Mark 5.

cauliflower curry

phool kopi jhhol

This is a very easy curry to make. Cauliflower is a great, no-waste vegetable. Do use the central stalk – it has a fine nutty flavour. Serve the curry with green or yellow split pea dal, some raita and chappatis or rice

SERVES 4

1 medium cauliflower
2 tbsp sunflower oil
1 large onion, finely chopped
2 cloves garlic, crushed
2 teaspoons ground cumin
½ teaspoon chilli powder or to taste
4 or 5 large tomatoes
salt

1 Break the cauliflower into fairly large florets. Chop the central stalk finely.

2 In a large frying pan heat the oil and fry the cauliflower briskly in the hot oil until browned. Remove the pieces and keep on one side.

3 In the same pan, fry the onion and garlic slowly until soft and starting to brown. Add the cumin and fry for a minute or so to bring out the flavour of the spice. Add the chilli powder and fry for another minute.

4 Transfer the mixture to a large pan.

5 Using a sharp knife make crossways slits in the tomatoes and then place in a bowl and cover with boiling water. Leave for 3–4 minutes and then remove from the water and peel off the skins. Quarter the tomatoes, remove the seeds and chop finely. Add the chopped tomatoes to the onion and spices mixture and season to taste.

6 Put the cauliflower florets on top of this thick reddish brown sauce. Mix in gently, cover the pan and simmer until the cauliflower is tender, removing or replacing the lid to keep the liquid level as desired. This will take only about 4–5 minutes.

7 Adjust seasoning and serve hot.

accompaniments

Chutneys are easy to make and worth it too, as their wonderful bursts of flavour add a whole extra dimension to the meal. Chutney comes from the Hindu word *chatni*, which means 'for licking', in the sense of smacking one's lips after having enjoyed a particularly scrumptious taste, which I think sums it up perfectly. Lip-smacking chutneys can be smooth or chunky, mild to eye-wateringly hot, and they can be made in a matter of minutes. There are some great fresh chutneys as well as cooked ones. Some cooked chutneys can be eaten immediately; others may need to be left for a week or more for the flavours to develop.

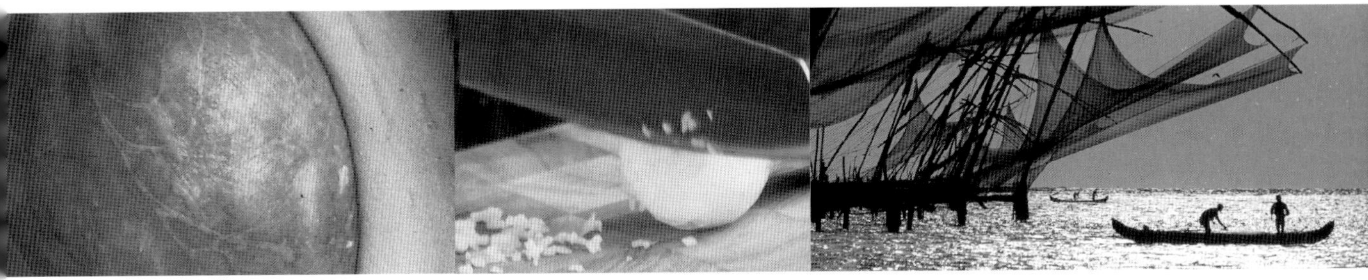

tomato and apricot chutney with tamarind

Tasty fresh chutneys such as this can be prepared quite quickly. They will also keep a few days in the fridge. This chutney is quite liquid in consistency, for a drier mixture, hold back some of the tomato juice when processing the ingredients.

250g (8oz) tomatoes
50g (2oz) dried apricots, finely chopped
1 fresh green chilli
1 tbsp tamarind paste
½ tsp ground coriander
salt
1 tsp sugar
juice of 1 lime, optional

1 Pierce the the tomato skins, cover them with boiling water, leave for 1–2 minutes, drain, skin and roughly chop.
2 Soak the chopped apricots in warm water for 1 hour, then drain.
3 Roast the green chilli for 10 minutes at 200°C (400°F) Gas Mark 6. Place in a polythene bag to cool and then peel and remove the seeds.
4 Process everything in a food processor until fairly smooth.
5 Season to taste and add a little lime juice if you wish.

avocado raita

Smooth, creamy with a hint of spice, this simple raita is a perfect foil for any vegetable curry.

1 ripe avocado
200g (7oz) thick yogurt
1 small tomato, deseeded and chopped
1–2 tbsp fresh coriander, finely chopped
3 spring onions, chopped
juice ½ lime
¼–½ tsp dried chilli flakes
1 tsp cumin seed
½ tsp coriander seed
salt and pepper

1 Peel the avocado, cut into small dice and blend with the yogurt until smooth.
2 Stir in the chopped tomato, fresh coriander and spring onions and mix well with the lime juice. In a small frying pan, dry-fry the chilli flakes, cumin seed and coriander seed until lightly toasted and then crush in a pestle and mortar or grind in a spice mill.
3 Stir into the avocado mixture and season to taste.

sugar snap peas with sambal

A sambal is a dressing that can be added to any vegetables. This dish can be served with rice and buttermilk or a rice pancake called *dosai* or *hoppers*.

SERVES 4

350g (12 oz) sugar snap peas
1 large onion, grated
1 clove of garlic, crushed
2 green chillies, finely minced or puréed
2.5cm (1 inch) root ginger, grated
2 tbsp sunflower oil
½ tsp cumin seed,
1 tsp ground turmeric
¼ tsp dried chilli flakes
250ml (8 fl oz) coconut milk
lemon juice to taste
salt

1 Cook the peas until just tender, drain and leave to cool.

2 Make a paste from the onions, garlic, chillies and ginger. Heat the oil in a large pan and fry the paste until well cooked.

3 Add the cumin seed, turmeric and chilli flakes and cook for a few minutes more, then remove the pan from the heat and stir in the coconut milk. Season to taste with salt and lemon juice.

4 Pour the sambal over the peas and serve at room temperature.

spiced potatoes with yogurt

dum aloo

Dum means 'to steam'. The traditional method for cooking ingredients in this way was to use a pot with a lid sealed with dough (*atta*) to prevent any steam escaping so that the entire dish retained all its flavour and aroma. The dish was then placed on a charcoal fire, sometimes with more coals on the lid to ensure all round cooking. In modern kitchens, the potatoes need to be cooked gently on the hob or in the oven, but what is important is to use a pan with a really good fitting lid so that the potatoes can cook in their own steam. Potatoes are an ideal ingredient to cook in this way as they easily absorb the flavour of all the spices while adding bulk and substance.

SERVES 4

2 tbsp oil
½ tsp brown mustard seeds
1 tsp cumin seeds
½ tsp turmeric
1 tsp ground coriander
450g (1lb) potatoes, peeled and cubed
1 tbsp tamarind pulp
1 tsp sugar
1 mild green chilli, deseeded and diced
75g (3oz) thick yogurt, beaten
salt

1 Heat the oil and fry the mustard and cumin seeds, add the turmeric and coriander and fry on a low heat until the spices are just toasted.

2 Add the potatoes and cook for 2–3 minutes turning frequently. Add 100ml (3½fl oz) water and salt and cook tightly covered for 15 minutes. Stir in the tamarind pulp, sugar and the mild chilli. Season to taste. Cook over a low heat until the potatoes are completely tender.

3 Whisk the yogurt with a fork and add very gradually to create a creamy sauce. Season to taste and serve hot.

spiced mushrooms with yogurt

kokur muttee dahiwali

Yogurt is not only served as a side dish or raita but is also cooked in many Indian dishes to make creamy sauces. It does have a tendency to curdle which will still taste fine but doesn't look so good. To avoid this, use a full fat yogurt, only add a little at a time on a low heat and it may help to beat it slightly first.

SERVES 2–4

2 tbsp ghee or oil
450g (1lb) button mushrooms, halved
1 tsp mustard seed
1 tsp coriander seed
1 tsp cumin
1/2 tsp chilli powder
1 clove garlic, crushed
175g (6oz) thick yogurt
salt

1 In a large frying pan, heat 1 tablespoon of ghee or oil and fry the mushrooms until just cooked and slightly browned. Transfer all the mushrooms and cooking juices to a plate and set aside.

2 Heat the other tablespoon of ghee or oil and fry the spices until lightly toasted, then sprinkle with salt and add the garlic and quickly fry for a minute on a high heat to release more of the juice.

3 Turn the heat down to very low and gradually stir in the yogurt a little at a time.

4 Continue adding the yogurt until the mixture is quite creamy and warmed through.

5 Adjust the seasoning and serve hot.

cabbage foogarth

This is a simple but delicious way to make a spiced vegetable side dish. It is great for cabbage but try aubergines (omit the coconut), carrots, runner beans, ladies fingers (okra), green bananas, tomatoes and unripened mangoes. You can also add half a teaspoon of cumin seed when frying the onions.

SERVES 4

1 small cabbage, finely chopped
2 tbsp sunflower or vegetable oil
1 tsp mustard seeds
1 large onion, finely sliced
2 cloves garlic, finely sliced
pinch of saffron
4 red or green fresh chillies, deseeded and cut lengthways
1-inch piece fresh ginger root, peeled and cut into 6 slices
1 tbsp freshly grated coconut, or desiccated coconut

1 Parboil the cabbage for 3–4 minutes and drain well.

2 In a pan heat the oil, add the mustard seeds and fry until they pop. Add the onion, garlic, saffron, chillies and ginger and fry until the onions are turning brown.

3 Add the drained cabbage to the fried mixture. Cook until the cabbage is just tender then stir in the fresh or desiccated coconut.

rice and milk dessert flavoured with rosewater

phirni

This recipe, given to me by Mamta, brought back memories of her childhood. She would know her grandmother was making phirni by the sight of the soaking unglazed earthenware bowls that were used as containers for the dessert. The bowls absorbed all the extra water from the pudding and gave it a velvety, creamy feel and scented the phirni with that special fragrance of the first rains.

SERVES 6

50g (2oz) basmati rice
2 tsp saffron
1 litre (1¾ pints) milk
150g (5oz) sugar
1 tsp green cardamom powder
2 tsp rosewater or 2 drops rosewater concentrate
2 tbsp flaked almonds
12 pistachios, chopped

1 Rinse rice in running water. Soak for 30 minutes. Drain, add 2 tablespoons of water and process in a blender to make a fine paste.

2 Dissolve the saffron in 1 tablespoon of warm milk.

3 Heat the rest of the milk in a pan, add the rice paste and sugar. Stir with a whisk. Reduce heat to low, until rice is cooked. Blend the mixture until it is a smooth, custard consistency. Add the saffron, cardamom powder and rosewater. Stir and remove.

4 Pour into individual bowls and refrigerate until chilled and well set.

5 Decorate with flaked almonds and chopped pistachio nuts.

asia pacific

This is a region of culinary contrasts, from the complete simplicity of Japanese food to the rich and complex spice dishes of Indonesia. There are many common threads, most notably the ubiquitous stir-fry, which has now been adopted extensively in the West. Rice, noodles and the soya bean in its many guises (soy sauce, tofu and miso) appear in the various cuisines in countless ways. Key flavourings are coconut, lemon grass, lime leaves, galangal and ginger.

I have included spicy soup from Thailand, refreshing salads from Indonesia, quick stir-fries from China and featherlight appetizers from Japan, together with some general food notes about these countries. Pages 188–189 detail some of the ingredients used in this part of the world. Thankfully, most are now available from large supermarkets, but it is also worth tracking down specialist shops. Ingredients are often much cheaper and you'll probably find a far bigger range, plus some expert advice on hand!

china

China, a great landmass of plains and mountain, lakes and deserts, naturally has a vast range of differing styles of cooking. The majority of the land is used for cultivation, especially rice, wheat, millet and the soya bean. Very little land is suitable for dairy cattle, which is why so few milk-based products are produced.

In the northern areas, the food tends to be more substantial to help people cope with the extremes of winter. Dumplings and noodles are the staple here, rather than rice, and the food tends generally to be saltier and spicier. Rice is eaten throughout the rest of China, served simply to accompany savoury meals, or occasionally cooked with eggs, such as in fried rice which I've included on page 208, a delicious meal in its own right. In China's central band with the provinces of Sichuan and Hunan, the cuisine is notable for its hot spicy food (perhaps a way to counteract the persistent gloomy damp and fogs) and fiery ginger chilli sauces. To the east around Shanghai, the seasonings tend to be sweeter, with mixtures of soy sauce and sugar as well as classic sweet-sour combinations. In Canton, typical cooking techniques include stir-frying, as in the cashew and ginger stir-fry on page 210.

indonesia

This is a richly spiced and varied cuisine reflecting the diverse nature of the many islands and its numerous invaders. As well as being influenced by a number of the world's major religions, it has also been in the hands of the Chinese, Portuguese, French, English and Dutch. The conquerors and traders over the centuries have brought a wide range of culinary traditions.

Fiery chillies are tempered with aromatic herbs and mixtures of sweet, sour and salty flavourings. Soft rice contrasts with crisp accompaniments such as fresh salad – for example, in the tasty combination on page 207, where the rice is served with a crunchy salad of cucumber and peanuts flavoured with coriander, lime and chilli. Rice is the foundation for every meal, with usually a couple of contrasting side dishes, one fairly liquid, the other drier.

japan

Japanese food is still heavily influenced by the seasons. Great emphasis is placed on freshness and it is usual to shop on a daily basis. Traditional dishes are often simple and beautifully presented. Two of my favourites are sushi and tempura, which can easily be made to look colourful and appetizing. Japanese noodles and vegetables are often cooked in water or stock, such as *dashi*, and thin soups are served frequently. Steaming is another very common cooking technique used to cook a range of vegetables such as carrots and green beans. Vegetable side dishes are quite simple, concentrating on one main flavour, such as the spinach with sesame on page 213. Few dairy products are used by the Japanese and much of the protein consumed is from vegetable sources, for example tofu. I've included a few different ways of cooking tofu in this section, such as the recipe on page 192 where the tofu is marinated and served with a savoury dipping sauce. Mineral-rich seaweed is used as a flavouring and garnish. Rice, plainly served, is a staple, but noodles are also common, often served hot in a soup or chilled for noodle dishes in summer. I've included a selection of noodle dishes, using fine egg noodles and rice noodles.

thailand

The basic Thai flavourings are complex mixtures that range from the subtle to the explosive. The Thai use chillies in almost every conceivable way – fresh, dried, whole, chopped, crushed or sliced into rings, as well as large amounts of sharp-flavoured ingredients, such as lime juice and tamarind juice (made by soaking tamarind pulp in water), to wake up the taste buds. These hot and sour flavours need tempering with sweetness and saltiness, and soy sauce and palm sugar or sugar are frequently used. The trick is to create a balance of flavours in the initial spice paste. I was lucky enough to see these pastes being prepared in Bangkok and Chiang Mai, watching endless chopping, crushing and pounding. No weighing scales in sight of course, but years of experience! You'll find a 'starter' spice paste on page 189. My advice is to go easy on the chillies, gradually increasing the amount you use to get the right heat for your palate.

Tom yam, the traditional soup, is hot, but several of the other dishes I have included have much more restrained spicing, such as the refreshing green papaya salad on page 212. Rice and noodles provide staple fillers. Noodles are served as an accompaniment to a simple vegetable mix, such as on page 204, but can also be an integrated part of the dish, as in the stir-fry with vermicelli on page 211. For any stir-fry, preparation is the key, so make sure everything is ready prior to cooking.

common ingredients and useful techniques

bamboo shoots
The tender shoots of the bamboo are cut when they are about 15cm (6 inches) above ground. Available canned, they are used in stir-fries and other vegetable dishes.

basil – holy and sweet
Holy basil is a darker green than sweet basil and has a distinctive aniseed flavour. It is used in Thai cooking and added at the end of cooking for flavour and garnish.

bean sprouts
Buy fresh white sprouts or grow your own from the mung bean. These are good in salads or briefly cooked in a stir-fry to keep their light and crisp qualities. Keep them bagged in the refrigerator for up to 3 days.

coconut
See pages 190–191.

curry leaves
Sold dried and fresh, these small olive-green leaves add a fresh aromatic taste.

galangal
Looks similar to ginger, but with a pinker tinge and a more astringent flavour. Bought either fresh or dried. It needs to be peeled and sliced before using.

ginger
Used throughout the Orient. The root is peeled, sliced thinly, diced, slivered, crushed or grated. It has a refreshing, pungent, citrus-like taste with a fiery hint, and is good for the digestion. Pickled ginger (*see page 199*) is used in Japanese sushi.

kaffir lime (fruit and leaves)
The kaffir lime is like a common lime, but with a dark knobbly skin. The dark green, glossy leaves add an intense floral lemon-lime flavour to a dish.

horseradish (wasabi)

This is an essential Japanese condiment. It comes from a small green plant that grows in clear mountain streams. The root is prized for its fiery flavour, and wasabi is traditionally served with sushi, soba and other noodle dishes. A small amount adds considerable bite. You can buy wasabi as a powder or a paste.
A powder needs to be reconstituted with lukewarm water prior to using.

lemon grass

Lemon grass stalks add an intense lemon flavour and scent to Thai and Indonesian cooking. The stalks, which are usually sold in bundles, are about the same size and length as spring onions, but they are hard skinned and fibrous. Trim off the ends and any outer layers that are tough. One stalk should yield about 2–3 tablespoons of finely chopped lemon grass. Keep in the refrigerator for 2–3 weeks or freeze.

miso

Miso is a condiment made from a fermented mixture of soya beans, grain (rice or barley), salt and water. It varies widely in flavour, colour, texture and aroma. Use it to flavour soups, stews, casseroles and sauces.

mushrooms

Common varieties include Black mushrooms (Wood Ear or Cloud Ears), Enoki, Shiitake and Straw. All dried mushrooms will need rehydrating in hot water before slicing and cooking. Use any soaking water for stock.

noodles

See pages 200–201.

palm sugar

A thick sticky sugar with a fudge-like flavour sold in tubs and blocks. If unavailable, use soft dark brown sugar.

rice

Rice is invariably white, can be short-, medium- or long-grained and tends to be cooked without salt. Sticky rice, used for a traditional pudding on page 216, is a particular type of rice that is also called glutinous rice.

sesame oil

A strongly flavoured aromatic oil made from the roasted seeds. Use to marinate or sprinkle on food before serving.

soy sauce

Made from fermented soya beans and salt, sometimes with the addition of wheat or barley, soy sauce adds colour, flavour, sweetness and saltiness.

tamarind pulp

This has a sour lemony taste. Ready-made paste has a good flavour and is convenient. The block form must be soaked and strained to extract the thick juice. Pour over hot water to dissolve the block, sieve out the seeds and any other bits, then use the thick sauce that remains.

tofu

Tofu or bean curd is made from coagulated soya milk and sold in blocks. Silken tofu is soft and creamy textured; firm tofu is denser and good for stir-fries and marinades.

water chestnuts

Sold in cans, this crisp, sweet-tasting walnut-size bulb can be eaten raw or lightly cooked in stir-fries.

stir-frying

A technique used throughout Asia. A wok is essential. This is a wide, round-based, thin metal frying pan which heats up quickly and provides a good cooking surface. When stir-frying, prepare everything in advance, do all the chopping and have sauces and dips ready, noodles soaked, and so on. Always add the slowest-cooking ingredients first.

spice pastes

Many spice pastes are commercially available which saves time, but strict vegetarians need to look out for ingredients such as shrimp paste or salted fish. I prefer making a large quantity in a food processor and freezing it in tablespoon-sized purées in ice-cube trays. A pestle and mortar can be used. The flavour is good, but it does take time and patience.

FOR A BASIC HOT SPICE PASTE

6–8 chillies (see page 21 for chilli preparation)
3 cloves garlic, crushed
2 small shallots, finely chopped
1 tbsp galangal or root ginger, grated
2 tsp coriander seed, crushed
1 stick lemon grass, finely chopped
2 tsp lime rind, chopped
1 tsp salt

Pound or grind everything to a thick paste. It is unpleasant to taste this raw so, if you are wary of chillies, make the mix with half the chillies suggested and then alter the quantities the next time if you prefer a hotter mix.

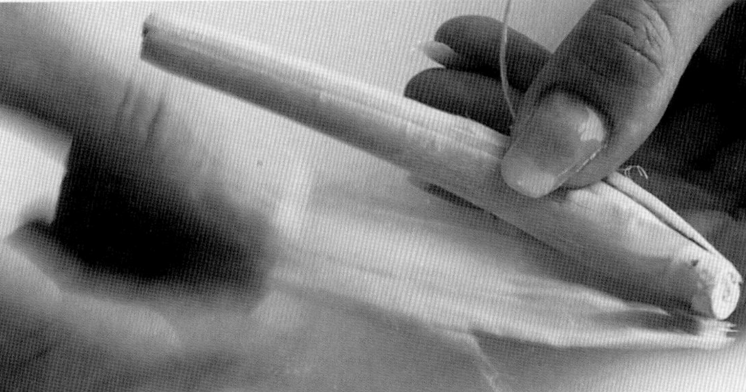

coconut

Coconut trees grow around the world in lowland, tropical and subtropical habitats. Coconut, or rather coconut milk, is used throughout Asia as an ingredient in both sweet and savoury recipes. It is used in soups, curries, dressings and all kinds of desserts. I love its unmistakable flavour and richness. Fresh coconuts are widely available, as are many coconut products such as coconut milk, coconut cream, block creamed coconut and desiccated coconut.

fresh coconut

In Asian countries, fresh coconut is obviously plentiful and a coconut grater is standard equipment in most households. It is possible to grate coconut safely using a rotary hand grater.

Buy a fresh coconut with plenty of liquid inside as it is likely to be fresher. Pierce the shell of the coconut through the 'eyes', the round bald patches near the top, and then drain off the clear liquid. (This is good to drink.) Crack open the shell using a mallet or hammer. Cut away the white flesh and peel or cut off any thin dark brown skin, cut the flesh into chunks, then grate or chop into small pieces. One medium-size coconut should provide 3–4 cups. Keep the grated flesh in air-tight plastic bags or containers in the refrigerator for a maximum of 4 days.

coconut milk

Coconut milk is not the clear liquid inside a coconut. The coconut milk used in cooking is the milky liquid extracted from the grated flesh of mature fresh coconuts or reconstituted from desiccated coconut (dried shredded coconut).

You can make coconut milk from fresh coconut following the instructions below, or you can buy coconut milk from good supermarkets and specialist shops. If you are using ready-made canned coconut milk, it may need diluting with a little water as some brands are extremely thick.

To make coconut milk in a blender or food processor: measure a couple of cups of grated coconut and add 2½ cups of hot water. Process for about 30 seconds, then strain through a fine sieve or piece of muslin, pressing with your hand or the back of a spoon to squeeze out all the moisture. Put the coconut back into the processor and add another 2½ cups hot water, then blend and strain again.

To make coconut milk by hand, put 2 cups grated coconut in a large bowl and pour over 2½ cups hot water. Leave to soak until the mixture is lukewarm, then mash or knead by hand for a few minutes and strain through a fine sieve or a piece of muslin, squeezing out as much liquid as possible. Tip the coconut back into the bowl and add another 2½ cups hot water and repeat the process.

With both methods, the first milk produced will be thick and very creamy while the second batch will be much thinner. Sometimes coconut cream is specified, especially for desserts; in that case use milk from the first batch. If you leave this to stand, a rich layer rises to the top which has a very creamy consistency.

block creamed coconut

This looks like a solid brick of white fat. It can be added directly into a recipe in chunks, although grating makes it easier to incorporate. I find a block of cream coconut is useful for enriching a soup or stew quite quickly towards the end of cooking, rather like stirring in some ordinary cream.

To make coconut milk from block coconut, grate the block and dilute with boiling water to produce a coconut milk: 200g (7oz) creamed coconut will make about 600ml (20fl oz/2½ cups) of thickish coconut milk. To make a coconut cream simply use less water.

desiccated coconut

This is very finely grated dried coconut flesh. To reconstitute, pour over some boiling water, then strain. This is certainly faster than using a fresh coconut, though the flavour is not quite the same.

sesame tofu with dipping sauce

shoga aji no tofu

Tofu marinated in a simple mix of soy sauce, garlic, ginger and sugar. Serve as a great starter with this dipping sauce, or try the one on page 195.

SERVES 4

2 packets tofu, each 280g (9oz)

FOR THE MARINADE

5 tbsp Japanese soy sauce
1–2 tbsp sugar
2 tbsp rice wine or mirin
1 tbsp grated root ginger
2 cloves garlic, finely chopped

50g (2oz) plain flour
40g (1½oz) sesame seeds
2 tbsp sunflower oil
3 spring onions, finely chopped, to garnish

FOR THE DIPPING SAUCE

2 tbsp soy sauce
2 tbsp rice or cider vinegar
½ tsp sugar
2 tbsp chopped fresh coriander

1 Drain the tofu and press dry with a kitchen towel. Cut the tofu into thick slices or rough cubes.

2 Mix the ingredients for the marinade in a large bowl and then marinate the tofu for 30 minutes occasionally basting or turning the pieces.

3 Mix together the flour and the sesame seeds. Coat each piece of tofu in this mixture prior to frying.

4 Heat the oil and fry the coated tofu in batches until crisp and brown. Keep each batch warm.

5 Mix the ingredients for the dipping sauce together well.

6 Serve sprinkled with the spring onions and the dipping sauce.

COOK'S TIP *Use less sugar if you don't want the marinade to be too sweet.*

thai fruit salad

yam polamai

Sharp and sweet notes contrast in this refreshing salad. Use it as a side dish, or serve it as a starter. You can vary the fruit selection but pick fruits that keep their texture, avoid banana or strawberry that quickly soften or discolour.

SERVES 4

75g (3oz) red grapes, halved
75g (3oz) green grapes, halved
1 orange
125g (4oz) lychees
75g (3oz) water chestnuts
2 slices pineapple
50g (2oz) cashew nuts lightly toasted
for the dressing
½ tsp salt or to taste
1 tsp sugar
2 tbsp lime juice
1 tbsp finely chopped fresh coriander

FOR THE GARNISH
slivers of garlic and shallots
oil for deep frying

1 Halve the grapes and deseed. Peel the orange by removing the top and bottom and then the peel and pith using a serrated knife. Pull the orange apart into small shreds. Chop the lychees. Slice the water chestnuts into neat ovals. Peel the pineapple and remove any 'eyes' or tough core and chop into small cubes.

2 Mix all the prepared fruit together in a decorative bowl and stir in the cashew nuts.

3 For the dressing, dissolve the salt and sugar in the lime juice and stir gently with the coriander into the fruit.

4 For the garnish, deep fry thin slivers of garlic and shallot until golden brown.

tempura vegetables with dipping sauce

tempura yasai

These traditional crispy nibbles from Japan are extremely easy to make. Choose a variety of vegetables for contrast, such as: green beans, asparagus cauliflower, carrots, broccoli, courgette and mushrooms. Don't be nervous about making batter as a thin lumpy batter gives the best result. Make up as much as you need as it keeps. The dipping sauce is very simple: for a more sour flavoured dipping sauce, add a little ready-made tamarind, or for a more fiery taste, add a few chilli flakes, or slivers of ginger.

SERVES 4–6

FOR THE BATTER

1 egg
250ml (8fl oz) ice cold water
125g (4oz) plain flour
½ tsp salt (optional)
1kg (2lb) vegetables of your choice (see above for suggestions)
vegetable oil for deep frying
lemon wedges (optional)

DIPPING SAUCE

1 tbsp soy sauce
1 tbsp mirin or rice wine
1 tsp sugar
2 tbsp water

1 Using a balloon whisk, beat the egg and water together and then whisk in the flour and salt if using. Do not beat more than necessary as a slightly lumpy batter gives a crisper end result.

2 Prepare vegetables of your choice by chopping or trimming into manageable bite-sized pieces and pat dry if necessary.

3 Pour oil to a depth of 2.5-cm (1-inch) in a deep small frying pan and heat until a piece of batter dropped in rises to the surface immediately. Coat a few pieces of vegetable at a time in the batter and then drop in the hot oil. Cook until golden brown.

4 Drain and serve with the dipping sauce or with lemon wedges and salt.

TIMESAVER *Both the dipping sauce and the batter can be prepared in advance.*

spiced thai soup

tom yam

Many Asian recipes start with the spices being crushed or pounded into a paste. It is worth doing a little chopping, crushing or grating first so that your food processor doesn't have to work too hard.Once the paste is made the rest of the soup is easily made. This recipe is hot. For a less powerful version cut down on the peppercorns and use a mild rather than a strong chilli.

SERVES 4–6

1–2 tsp peppercorns
2 cloves garlic
3 tbsp chopped coriander stalks1 green chilli, deseeded and diced
1 tsp grated fresh ginger root
3 stalks lemon grass, very finely chopped
900ml (1½ pints) vegetable stock
3 tbsp lime juice
2 carrots, peeled and diced
2 fresh cobs sweetcorn, kernels stripped
2 tbsp finely chopped fresh coriander leaves
1 tsp miso, dissolved in a little stock
salt

1 Grind the peppercorns and crush the garlic and put into a small food processor, spice mill or pestle and mortar with the coriander stalks, chilli, ginger and lemon grass and process or crush to a fine paste.

2 Put the paste, stock and lime juice in a large pan, bring to the boil and simmer for 10 minutes.

3 Add the carrot and sweetcorn kernels and simmer for 30 minutes or until the carrot is tender.

4 Just before serving stir in the fresh coriander and dissolved miso. Season with a little salt if necessary.

sushi with pickled ginger

Sushi make attractive and tasty appetizers which are easy and fun to make. You can create your own fillings with all sorts of vegetables. Cook any that are likely to be too crunchy. Fukusa sushi is also worth making. Use the same sushi rice and mix with chopped carrot, green beans, mushrooms and avocado. Wrap these in very thin omelettes and finish off with a strip of nori.

SERVES 4–6

250g (8 oz) Japanese sushi rice
350 ml (12 fl oz) water
½–1 tsp salt
½–1 tsp sugar
2 tsp rice wine vinegar
4 sheets nori
50–75g cucumber, cut in strips
50–75g orange or yellow red pepper, cored, deseeded and cut in strips
50–75g avocado, cut in slices

FOR THE GINGER

125g (4 oz) root ginger
125 ml (4 fl oz) rice wine vinegar
2 tbl sugar
¼ tsp salt

TO SERVE

soy sauce

1 To make the pickled ginger, peel and slice the ginger very finely. Boil the rice wine vinegar with sugar and salt. Pour over the ginger and leave overnight.

2 Cook the rice in the water for 10 minutes and then leave to stand for 15 minutes without removing the lid.

3 Dissolve the salt and sugar in the rice wine vinegar and while the rice is still warm, stir in this mixture. Adjust the seasoning as necessary.

4 Spread each nori sheet with a portion of rice. Cover with a selection of vegetable strips and roll up. Leave to rest in the refrigerator for 3–4 hours for the nori to soften.

5 Slice each roll to make 5–6 little rolls and serve with some pickled ginger and shoyu.

TIMESAVER *The pickled ginger can be made several days in advance.*

noodles

Noodles are used extensively in Asian cookery. They vary according to the type of flour used, come in a range of widths and all are fairly quick to cook. I find noodles are a versatile ingredient and use them in soups, stir-fries and with sauces. Try them hot or cold.

A popular and versatile cooking ingredient, noodles are used predominately in Asian cuisine.

chinese noodles

Noodles have been a staple food in China for thousands of years. Originally they were made by hand using a highly skilled technique involving holding the stretched-out paste in both hands and whirling it around several times. Then the paste was laid out on a board and folded and refolded repeatedly, before eventually turning into long, thin noodles. While in China today it is still possible to watch vendors make hand-pulled noodles, most noodles are made by machine for speed and convenience. Chinese noodles vary in width, but are usually served long and uncut, symbolizing long life according to Chinese tradition.

Noodles can be eaten either hot or cold, steamed, stir-fried, deep-fried, boiled or served in a soup. In some dishes, the stir-fry ingredients are served over noodles that have been prepared separately. In other recipes, the cooked or soaked noodles are tossed in the wok and mixed with other ingredients during the final stages of cooking. This allows the noodles to pick up more flavour from the sauce.

wheat-flour noodles

These noodles may be made with or without eggs. They were originally a staple food in the north of China where wheat takes precedence over rice. Wheat noodles can be white or yellow, thin like spaghetti or thick and flat.

egg noodles

The egg content gives these wheat-flour noodles a distinctive yellow colour. They are sold fresh or dried, in a number of widths and shapes, from the thinner vermicelli to flat, thicker noodles. Used in soups and stir-fries, they need to be boiled before using.

rice noodles

Made with rice flour and water, a large variety of rice noodles is available, from fine rice vermicelli to the thick, broad, flat noodles used in stir-fries and heartier soups. The term 'rice sticks', which usually means thin rice vermicelli, can sometimes describe thicker, flatter noodles. Rice noodles should be soaked in hot water for several minutes before using.

cellophane noodles

Also called glass noodles or vermicelli, cellophane noodles are made from mung-bean paste. Before using, soak them in hot (not boiling) water. Cellophane noodles work well in soups and stir-fries, absorbing the flavour of the other ingredients. They can also be deep-fried and will puff up and become quite crispy.

thai noodles

These are similar to the noodles described above, with broad and thin rice noodles, egg noodles and a transparent noodle made from soya-bean flour. Noodles are served with a variety of dressings.

The classic dish *pad Thai* is made with a stir-fry of bean curd, egg, flat noodles, peanuts, bean sprouts and a simple sauce of chilli, soy and lemon juice.

japanese noodles

In Japan there are two kinds of traditional noodles – udon and soba.

Udon noodles are made from wheat flour. They are thick noodles and are always served in soup.

Soba noodles are made from buckwheat, a distinctive dark-coloured grain. These noodles are brown in colour, thin and flat, and have a slightly nutty flavour.

Chilled noodles are very popular in Japan in summer and are easy to make. Boil the noodles in a large pan for 7–10 minutes or until soft, then rinse in cold water. Just before serving, plunge the noodles into ice-cold water, drain, then dress with shredded seaweed. Serve the cold noodles with a dipping sauce made from stock, soy sauce and rice wine.

chinese noodles with bean sprouts

chao miàn

In northern China, wheat is the staple grain so dishes from that region tend to include noodles rather than rice. Here the noodles are prepared separately and the other ingredients stir-fried and then served on top with the sauce.

SERVES 2–4

FOR THE SAUCE

1 tsp cornflour
250ml (8fl oz) vegetable stock
2 tbsp soy sauce
2 tbsp rice wine or dry sherry
1 tsp salt
1 tsp sugar

350g (12oz) egg noodles

FOR THE STIR-FRY

3 tbsp sunflower or peanut oil
1 clove garlic, finely chopped
2.5-cm (1-inch) piece ginger root, grated
2 shallots finely chopped
50g (2oz) button mushrooms, sliced
250g (8oz) pak choi, sliced
125g (4oz) bean sprouts
2 carrots, cut into matchsticks

1 Dissolve the cornflour in a little stock. Stir in the rest of the stock and mix in the soy sauce, rice wine, salt and sugar.

2 Cook the noodles in a large pan of boiling water for 3 minutes or until just tender, drain and keep warm.

3 Heat the oil in a wok or large frying pan and cook the garlic, ginger and shallots. Add all the remaining vegetables and stir fry for 1–2 minutes. Pour over the sauce and continue cooking until the sauce thickens.

4 Pile the noodles onto a large serving plate and pour over the vegetable sauce and serve hot.

COOK'S TIP *When stir-frying, always prepare all the vegetables before you start to cook.*

spiced tofu and sugar snap peas with noodles

pad thai jay

This dish is slightly less fiery but with the delicious bite of tamarind which goes well with the bland tofu and crisp sugar snap peas. This serves two people for a main course and four as a light snack.

SERVES 2–4

2 tsp miso
2 tbsp tamarind pulp
1 tbsp tomato purée
1 tbsp sugar
280g (9oz) tofu (approximately)
3 cloves garlic
3 spring onions, finely chopped
1 stalk lemon grass, finely chopped
1 red chilli, deseeded and finely chopped
1 tbsp grated ginger root
3 tbsp sunflower oil
200g (7oz) sugar snap peas
250g (8oz) rice or egg noodles

1 For the marinade, mix the miso with 2 tablespoons of water then stir in the tamarind, tomato purée and sugar.

2 Drain the tofu and press down between two pieces of kitchen paper, then slice or cube and coat the tofu with the marinade. Leave for 30 minutes or so turning over occasionally.

3 Pound the garlic with the spring onions, lemon grass, chilli, ginger root and sunflower oil.

4 Cook the noodles, drain and keep warm.

5 Using a wok or large frying pan, fry the spring onion and spice paste for 2–3 minutes then add the tofu and sugar snap peas. Fry for 2–3 minutes.

6 Stir in the drained cooked noodles. There should be enough moisture in the noodles for the sugarsnap peas to finish cooking. Serve immediately.

indonesian yellow rice with spiced cucumber

nasi kunint

Colourful, richly flavoured and simple to make, this rice is delicious served with a contrasting hot, sharp salad of cucumber. Make the salad first so that it can marinate while you prepare the rice.

SERVES 4

FOR THE SALAD

- 1 medium cucumber
- 1 tsp miso
- 1 tbsp palm sugar
- 2 tbsp lime juice
- 1/4 tsp chilli flakes
- 50g (2oz) roasted peanuts, crushed
- 1 shallot, sliced
- 50g (2oz) fresh coriander leaves, chopped

FOR THE RICE

- 400ml (14fl oz) coconut milk
- 1 stalk lemon grass
- 2 shallots, finely chopped
- 1/4 tsp grated nutmeg
- 1/2 tsp turmeric
- 3 cloves
- 1 bay leaf
- 250g (8oz) basmati rice
- salt

1 For the spiced cucumber, peel the cucumber, slice in half lengthways, remove any seeds and cut into 1-cm (1/2-inch) chunks.

2 Dissolve the miso and sugar in the lime juice and then mix well with the chilli, crushed peanuts, shallots, and coriander leaves.

3 Marinate for 30 minutes.

4 For the yellow coconut rice, mix the coconut milk with an equal quantity of water in a large pan. Add all the spice ingredients and bring the mixture to the boil. When boiling add the rice, then turn down the heat, cover and simmer for 20 minutes.

5 Uncover and fork through the rice adding a little hot water if necessary, then cook covered for a further 5 minutes or until just tender.

6 Serve the rice with the spiced cucumber separately or as a garnish.

COOK'S TIP *The richness of this dish will depend on the type of coconut milk. If it is very thick, water it down, otherwise the coconut can separate. Add a little water at the end of cooking to give the finished dish a smoother look.*

chinese vegetable fried rice

chaofàn

Most vegetables can be chopped and stir-fried and mixed into egg fried rice. I've suggested green beans, peas and mushrooms but you can also use peppers, bean sprouts or carrots. It is also a good way to use those up. You can serve this dish on its own, or with some pickled vegetables.

SERVES 4

250g (8oz) basmati rice, brown or white
4 eggs
4 tbsp sunflower or peanut oil
3 spring onions, finely chopped
1 clove garlic, crushed
2.5-cm (1-inch) ginger root, grated
1 tsp fennel seed
175g (6oz) green beans, sliced
175g (6oz) peas
125g (4oz) field mushrooms or chestnut mushrooms
1 tbsp soy sauce
salt and pepper

1 Measure the rice and boil it in double its volume of water. Once boiling cover the pan and cook for 10 minutes depending on the type of rice used. Brown basmati will take about 25 minutes to cook. Drain if necessary and leave to cool.

2 Lightly beat the eggs.

3 Heat 2 tablespoons of oil in the wok or large frying pan, when hot add the spring onion, garlic, ginger and fennel seed and stir-fry for about 1 minute, then add the green beans, peas and mushrooms and stir-fry for 2 minutes. Then push all the cooked vegetables to the side of the pan. Add a little more oil and pour in the beaten egg then stir a little to create a soft scrambled egg. Then mix in the stir-fried vegetables and the cooked rice. Continue to stir until the ingredients are evenly mixed. Season to taste.

4 Transfer into a large bowl and serve sprinkled with soy sauce. Serve hot.

TIMESAVER *For this dish, the rice can be cooked well in advance.*

stir-fry with cashew nuts and ginger

chao yaoguo

Light and fragrant this is an easy dish to prepare and can of course be varied to suit the vegetables available. As with all stir-frying, it is vital to assemble everything first so that once the cooking begins all the ingredients are ready prepared and to hand. For stir-frying, it is best to use a wok as there is plenty of cooking surface to get hot and you can stir vigorously. If you don't have a wok, choose a large fairly thin frying pan.

SERVES 2

prepared rice or noodles, ready for serving
2 tbsp soy sauce
2 tbsp dry sherry
juice ½ lemon
2 tsp sesame oil
2 tbsp sunflower oil
4 medium spring onions, cut on the diagonal
1 clove garlic, finely chopped
2 tbsp ginger root, cut in very fine matchsticks
125g (4oz) broccoli, divided into small florets
125g (4oz) baby corn, halved widthways
125g (4oz) asparagus, sliced on the diagonal
125g (4oz) bamboo shoots
125–175g (4–6oz) cashew nuts

1 Mix together the soy sauce, dry sherry, lemon juice and sesame oil

2 Using a wok or a large thin frying pan, heat 1 tablespoon of sunflower oil and quickly fry the cashew nuts until lightly browned. Transfer to a plate.

3 Heat the other tablespoon of oil in the wok and quickly fry the spring onions, garlic and ginger, then add the prepared vegetables, one type at a time in the order in which they are given in the recipe, that is starting with the broccoli, then baby corns followed by asparagus then bamboo shoots and fry each vegetable for a minute or so before adding the next one.

4 Toss in the cashew nuts and continue stir-frying, then pour over the sauce and cook for 1 minute.

5 Serve immediately with rice or noodles.

thai spiced stir-fry with fine egg noodles

ba mee so ba

This is a fiery stir-fry which needs a spice paste as its flavour base. If you are going to eat this type of food frequently it is worth investing in a sturdy food processor or spice mill and making plenty of paste at once. To save time, you can buy ready-made spice paste – red or yellow. Strict vegetarians should note that these pastes often include dried shrimp or salted fish, which is why I make my own.

SERVES 2–4

125g (4oz) fine egg noodles

FOR THE STIR FRY

2 tbsp peanut oil
2 tbsp spice paste (*page 189*)
2 shallots, finely chopped
1 stalk lemon grass, finely chopped
1 tsp galangal or ginger root, finely grated
2 red peppers, deseeded and finely sliced
250g (8oz) green beans
1 small aubergine, chopped
1 x 400g (14oz) can palm hearts
3 lime leaves
3 tbsp vegetable stock
3 tbsp soy sauce
1 tsp sugar

1 Break the noodles and soak in a bowl of warm water, drain, and set aside.

2 Heat the oil and fry the spice paste briefly then stir in the finely chopped shallots, lemon grass and galangal or ginger.

3 Next add the red peppers, green beans and aubergine, stirring and frying continuously for 2–3 minutes.

4 Then add the noodles, palm hearts, lime leaves, vegetable stock, soy sauce and sugar, and continue cooking until the noodles are tender.

5 Pile into a serving dish and serve immediately.

thai salad

papaya pok pok

Salads in Thailand are often served with sticky rice to make simple meals. The pale green, firm-fleshed papaya is often an ingredient which, though related to the salmon-coloured fruit, is quite different and often cooked.

SERVES 4–6

FOR THE DRESSING

4 cloves garlic, crushed
1 red chilli, deseeded and diced
2 tbsp palm sugar
juice of 3 limes

FOR THE SALAD

1 green papaya
½ cucmber
2 tbsp fresh coriander
2 tbsp fresh mint
2 tbsp fresh basil
2 tbsp spring onion, finely chopped

1 Prepare the salad dressing by mixing the ingredients together and stir until the sugar dissolves.

2 Peel the papaya and grate from the outside finely by hand on a coarse grater or mandolin. Avoid including the seeds.

3 Cut the cucumber in matchsticks.

4 Toss in the fresh herbs and just before serving, mix in the dressing.

COOK'S TIP *When grating the green papaya, take care not to include the seeds as they can cause stomach upsets. If you can't buy green papaya, try this salad dressing with other firm salad vegetables, such as carrots, radishes, spring onions, celery, and cucumber.*

sesame with spinach

shigimchee

Sesame is used as a condiment in Japan. It is roasted and ground with salt to make *goma sio*, a most delicious flavouring that is sprinkled over food. It is delicious sprinkled over vegetables such as aubergines, carrots, mushrooms, leeks, green beans or, here, used with spinach.

SERVES 2–4

3 tbsp of white sesame seeds
2 tbsp of sugar
2½ tbsp of shoyu (Japanese soy sauce)
500g (1¼lb) spinach
1 tbsp sunflower oil

1 To make the dressing, place the sesame seeds in a small pan and dry-fry over a medium flame, moving the pan constantly so that the seeds toast evenly and do not burn. Put the seeds in a pestle and mortar and grind to a fine powder, add the sugar and continue grinding until the mix has become very finely ground. Stir in the shoyu and mix well.

2 Wash and dry the spinach, then heat the oil in a large pan and briskly cook the spinach until it has just wilted. Put the spinach in a warm serving bowl and toss in the dressing. Serve hot or leave to cool.

spicy north-eastern mushroom salad with tofu

yam het

This is traditionally eaten with sticky rice (*see page 216*). The salad ingredients can be varied as the Thais are very much put-in-what-you-have cooks so you could add celery, carrots, shallots or other varieties of raw mushroom. I like to throw in some marinated spicy tofu.

SERVES 4

FOR THE TOFU

2 cloves garlic, crushed
1 dried red chilli
1 tsp black pepper
1 tsp ground coriander
2 tbsp soy sauce
1 tsp sugar

2 packets tofu approx 560g (1¼lb), cubed
1 tbsp sunflower or groundnut oil

FOR THE SALAD

1 garlic clove
3 small red chillies (or to taste)
1 tsp sugar
2 tbsp lemon juice
2 tbsp soy sauce
250g (8oz) button mushrooms sliced
75g (3oz) cucumber, sliced
4 spring onions, sliced
1 small red onion, halved and sliced
2 tbsp roasted peanuts, crushed
2 tsp sesame seeds
Chinese leaves for lining the dish (optional)
coriander leaves, to garnish

1 For the tofu marinade, crush the garlic, chop the chilli finely and grind the black pepper. Pound all the ingredients in a pestle and mortar. Add the ground coriander. Stir in the soy sauce and the sugar and pour over the tofu. Leave to marinate for up to an hour, turning over occasionally.

2 Heat the oil and fry the tofu until crisp then set aside.

3 For the salad, crush the garlic and chop the chillies finely and crush in a pestle and mortar. Mix together with the sugar, lemon juice and soy sauce to make a sauce.

4 In a large bowl mix together the sliced mushrooms, cucumber, spring onions and red onion.

5 Pour over the dressing and mix well.

6 Just before serving, mix in the spiced tofu and toss in the peanuts and sesame seed.

7 Serve plain or use Chinese leaves to line a plate or bowl and then fill with the salad. Garnish with coriander leaves.

mango fan with sticky rice

khaoneow mamuang

Glutinous rice has a high starch content which means that the grains do not separate as they cook but stick together slightly. It is easy to make as long as you have the right variety of rice and remember to prepare it in advance. Sticky rice is popular in Thailand, particularly for visitors and also in Thai restaurants all over the world. It is often served with a coconut cream which probably would not be the case in Thai homes, but is a very nice extra!

SERVES 4

TO PREPARE STICKY RICE
125g (4oz) glutinous rice
50g (2oz) sugar
250ml (8fl oz) water
2 mangoes
coconut cream

1 The day before, start preparing the sticky rice. Put the rice in a large bowl of water and leave for at least 3 hours or preferably overnight. Drain and rinse thoroughly. Line a steamer with muslin or cheesecloth and steam the rice for 30 minutes or until the grain is completely soft and can be pressed between the fingers, then turn into a bowl.

2 Dissolve the sugar in the water and then add the rice and simmer until the water is absorbed. Turn onto a plate and either press flat, cool, then cut into shapes, or fluff with a fork.

3 Peel and cut the mangoes in half using the stone as a guide, keeping your knife as close as possible to the oval stone. Cut the mango into slices and arrange in a fan, then place a little mound of sticky rice at the point of the fan and drizzle some coconut cream over the rice.

index

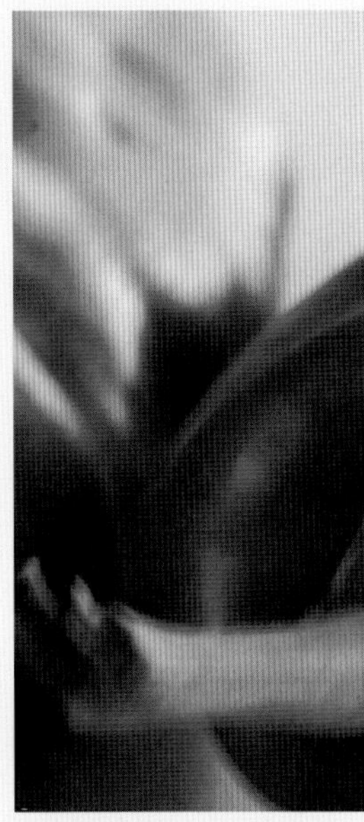

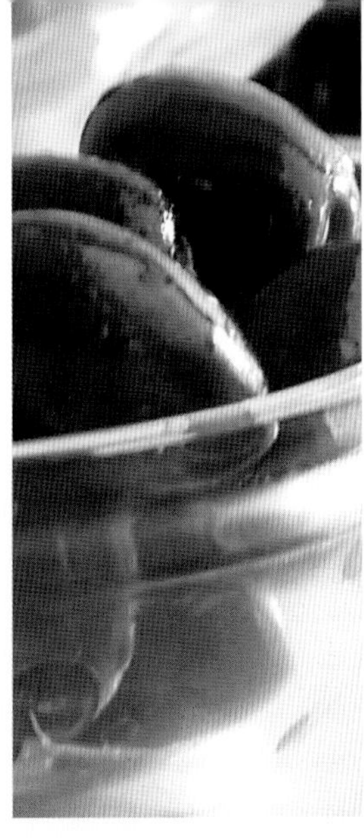

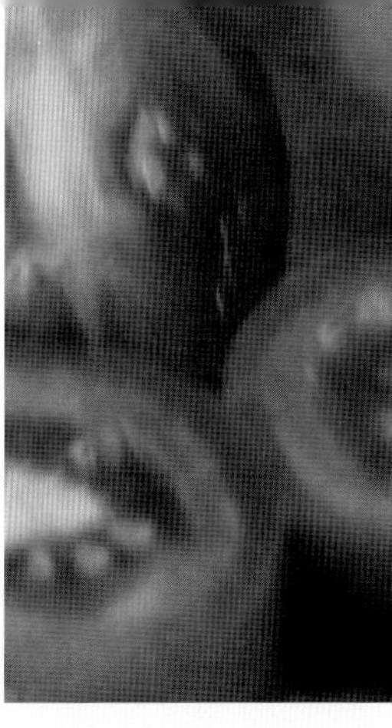

acknowledgements

I would like to thank everyone who has been so generous in giving me not only their family recipes but also much insight into their own particular style of cooking. It was a joy to listen to so many personal stories about food and its traditions. Starting work on a book with such a wealth of material made the cooking a delight and I finished writing this book feeling that my horizons had been truly expanded.

My sincere thanks to all of the following for their contributions: Beatrice Araevello, Fatima Bakali, Lorraine Buckley, Gerry Haliburn, Antonia Halse, Nawal Hassanyeh, Annette Heidrich, Edgar and Sharon Linares-Bowles, Barbara Majumdar, Mamta Dalal Mangaldas, Helen O'Malley, Garry Price and Michele Dubourdieu-Price, Rima Ferzoli, Laura Ferzoli, Zeynep Saglam, Poorna Shaw, Dan Schlesinger, Sutarti Suparno, Rania Giannopoulos.

Also thanks to Calvey Taylor-Haw for his beautiful photographs and all his hard work and sense of humour.

Last but not least thanks to two dear friends – Rachel Anderson and Rachel Skingsley, both highly talented exceptional individuals who worked tirelessly with me: cooking, shopping, inspiring and advising, all with a boundless enthusiam and a great sense of fun.

Picture credits

The publisher would like to thank the Steamer Trading Cookshop (in Lewes) and the Kitchenware Company (in Richmond) for very kindly supplying materials for the photoshoot.

We also thank the following picuture agencies for permission to use their images:

CORBIS pp. 2, Bob Krist; 22, Corbis, Bo Zaunders; 69, Barbara Peacock; 84, Owen Franken; 85, 88, Patrick Ward; 94, Reza; 120, Stuart Westmorland; 120, Owen Franken; 124, Michelle Garrett; 125, Johannes Armineh; 152, Dallas and John Heaton; 153, Chris Lisle; 187, Keren Su, Yang Liu; 190, Douglas Pebbles; 200, Kevin Christopher Ou.
IMAGE BANK p. 13, Tom Owen Edmunds.